TALES FROM THE END
OF THE BRIDGE

TALES
from the END
of the BRIDGE

Homer R. Ayers

PUBLISHING

First Edition

Printed in the United States of America

Library of Congress Control Number: 2009930066
ISBN-13: 978-0-9801862-4-6

Book and cover design: Mark S. Phillips

Wythe-North Publishing
P.O. Box 1208
Proctorville, Ohio 45669

www.wythe-north.com

ACKNOWLEDGEMENTS

Special thanks to MARILYN COOPER of COOPER GALLERY, 122 E. Washington, Lewisburg, West Virginia 24901 and to her husband, G.P. COOPER, the photographer, for granting permission to use the picture of the end of the old bridge in Alderson, West Virginia, for the cover of this book. Mr. Cooper, like the boys at the end of the bridge, obviously has a view of the end of the bridge, with all of it's beauty, that many of us miss.

Thanks to my secretary, Patsy Davidson, whose knowledge of the computer and sense of order were invaluable in writing this book.

Finally, my wife, Laura, must be acknowledged for limiting the number of stories in this book through her careful editing. Otherwise, the book would be twice its size and would surely offend half of my readers.

CONTENTS

Foreword x
1. My World. 1
2. The Barbershop. 5
3. When the Frog Got His Wings. 11
4. The Race that Never Was 17
5. The Chief. 21
6. The Little German 27
7. Looking For the Greener Grass 35
8. Camp Greenbrier 45
9. The Dog Breeders. 51
10. Com-Ah-Ne-Ah-Sa 59
11. The Ruby Red Cross 63
12. Big Man 69
13. The Recruiter 73
14. The Applefest Circa 1952 77
15. The Japanese Attack on Alderson, West Virginia. 81
16. The West Coast Pants 85
17. No More Yeas 89
18. Wire's Big Date 93
19. Ghosts in the Rear View Mirror 99
20. Crinoline and Playtex 107
21. Parrot. 111
22. The Bridge. 117
23. Shoes for Sale 123
24. Old Man Ed. 127
25. The Stove's Ah Dancin 133

FOREWORD

I cannot deny that a couple of the following stories were written before my son, Christopher, married. However, his first marriage brought about an epiphany—a vision that I would one day, and likely soon, become a grandfather. So, I began to write short stories for my grandchild, stories that would tell him or her something about my early life, growing up in rural Southern West "By God" Virginia when West Virginia was, indeed, West "By God" Virginia.

As I wrote, I realized that some of the stories went far beyond what a young child should read. Hell, some of them went beyond what my wife should read. Then, my grandson, Samuel Alan Ayers, was born. I rightly concluded that he could read these stories when he became an adult. As such, this book was written for and dedicated to Sam, with the love and understanding of my wife, Laura, my daughter, Shannon (now deceased) and my son, Christopher.

It is also dedicated to all of those young men who exchanged tall tales with me at the end of the bridge from circa 1948 to 1954. These men were not only my friends, they were my mentors. Without them, I, most likely, would have been without understanding and, most of all, humor. In that group there were two professors, three attorneys, a judge, several educators and coaches and others with specialized training beyond high school. When we meet, no mention is made of degrees and education; however, bachelor degrees, master degrees and even doctorate degrees are fairly common. Nevertheless, each of us is aware that we all received a part of our early education from guys who never graduated high school. This, in and of itself, is a banquet for thought.

Since I began this book, I acquired a new daughter-in-law,

Jackie, a step granddaughter, Madelyn and a baby granddaughter, Kathie Shannon Emerson Ayers—named for her mother's sister, my daughter and my wife's father, all deceased. We call her Emerson or Little "M." I suppose I will have to write another book for Emerson. Maybe *Tales Beyond the End of the Bridge*.

But, for now, please enjoy Sam's book.

H.R.

MY WORLD

In 1943, when child abuse was an unknown phrase, my second grade teacher, who used a ruler like a samurai warrior, arched her back and tilted her head slightly to the left, which was always a prelude to some major announcement. After a long pause, she pointed her ruler toward the class, waving it from right to left for effect, and said, "The world is round—not flat, like some of our earlier forefathers claimed." Her statement carried with it an air of undeniable truth and wisdom, as if she had just disclosed a secret only she, and now our entire class, knew.

"That's dumb," I thought. "Not my world." In my world there are mountains so high they brace the sky, keeping the moon and stars from falling—mountains that overlook a winding river, a river as wide as a football field or wider, in a valley that must have been chiseled by the hand of God. There are railroad tracks, hugging the south bank of the river, as though the two were happily married, with an old concrete bridge that joins the two sides of the river, forming the center of my world.

"God lives in those mountains," my mother said. I believed her then, as I still do. When I was a small boy, she showed me the face of God in the lightning, and we listened to God's angry voice in the thunder—a low bass voice that made an echo throughout the valley, telling man of His expectations and His displeasures.

During the most severe thunderstorms, which occurred mostly in the spring and early summer, my mother and I would hide under the bed, safe from the eyes of God, covering our ears in an effort to muffle the wrath of God. At the age of six or seven, I found a more peaceful God. My mother never did, but she did abandon her place under the bed and thereafter sat in a windowless stairwell until God's angry voice became a distant echo. Then, she would resume her work, as if nothing had happened.

Sometimes, the fog capped the mountains. At other times, the fog drifted over the valley, giving my world the appearance of a mystical village from another land, found only in fiction or the mind of a young boy. But when the fog lifted, the mystical village became reality, and the layers of dust covering the streets and houses from the coal driven railroad engines and the coal furnaces cloaked the buildings, masking the need for paint and repair. I chose to remain in the mystical village, surrounded by people whose lives were, from my perspective, real and fiction, like the old bridge, which was the focal point of my world.

The old bridge was built or reconstructed during the late 1920s, mostly by local workmen, probably employed by some government program designed to end the ravages of the great depression. It was then, and still is, one of the most beautiful bridges I have ever seen. The architecture, likely European—almost gothic, with four arches to accommodate the flow of the river below, survived the spring floods, the winter snows, the rattle of horses and wagons, the sounds of the old trucks and cars, and the pounding of bare feet, shoes and boots over the decades, while keeping her original grandeur for the sons and grandsons to follow. At the northwest corner of the old bridge, a sign read, "Alderson—Founded in 1777 by 'Elder' John Alderson, the frontier missionary...."

I know the exact location of all of the places in my world—places such as Snake Run, Wolf Creek, Possum Holler, Flat Mountain, Muddy Creek Mountain, Blaker's Mill, and, of course, the spring places, Fort Spring, Sweet Springs, Pence Springs, Blue Sulphur Springs and a host of others, visited by people, far and near, in the 1800s and the early part of the twentieth century, to drink water with the smell of rotten eggs and bathe in tubs or pools of the foul smelling liquid, ostensibly as a cure for colds, molds and sore assholes, or as some believed, as a preservative for longevity.

Camp Greenbrier for Boys, a facility where young boys could become a part of nature, living in tents with a wood floor, playing tennis, learning to shoot a rifle, and riding horseback, and The Women's Federal Prison, sometimes given names such as "Reformatory" or "Correctional Institution," rather than "Prison," to be politically correct, were in my world but were never a part of my world. I doubted that any of the young boys at the camp became a part of nature or that any of the inmates were reformed or corrected at this institution. Each place sent a clear message—"the locals weren't welcome." I didn't care. I simply didn't recognize them as a part of my world.

One of my favorite places was the railroad station. I met the trains frequently just to watch the people—those who were visiting the camp or the institution, a few locals, servicemen returning from the war, on leave or home permanently, without an arm or a leg or afflicted by other wounds, apparent or hidden, and a coffin or two containing those who were not lucky enough to lose just an arm or a leg or plagued with other problems, mental or physical, for the remainder of their lives. Sometimes, I wondered about which of those were the most fortunate.

Oh, there were places , somewhere on the outer reaches of my world—Bluefield, Beckley, Charleston, Huntington, Parkersburg and places in the other Virginia, such as Roanoke, Richmond and Lexington—but I never expected to see these places.

There were also places like New York, Boston, San Francisco, Atlanta and other cities, where people lived and worked in high rise buildings, without knowing their neighbors, but these were different worlds—worlds that I couldn't fully imagine.

Then, too, there were places such as London, Berlin, Paris and a myriad of small islands in the south Pacific—places marked on maps at the barbershop where the Dead Pecker Club, a number of old men who gathered throughout the day to plot the location of the local boys fighting either Germans or Japanese, to discuss the weather or to pass along a humorous tale, generally involving a local person. Those were the best stories.

Each night, except for those nights in the dead of winter when the freezing air sweeps through the valley, a group of young men would meet near the northwest corner of the bridge, at a billboard sign, with a wide ramp at the base, three or four feet from ground level, used by the billboard workmen for replacing advertisements and used by the boys from the end of the bridge, sometimes as a stage and sometimes as a couch or a row of seats. The wood of the ramp had become so smooth from constant use over the years that the signboard seemed to be a large piece of furniture, with a painting that changed periodically, like women change paintings in their homes.

When I reach puberty, I will be welcomed by the boys at the end of the bridge. Well, not really welcomed. Maybe tolerated would be a better word. Thereafter, the end of the bridge would become the central part of my world, a magical place where an impromptu theater was performed, first by one, then another, telling stories of yesterday or days gone by, making every story live and personal. These would be the original tales from the end of the bridge, told by the philosophers of my time—Red Bird, Wimpy, Bladder, Suicide, Squinch Eye or Backer Mouth, Bruiser, Nat, Buzzy, Mocas, Wire, Axehead, Boris or FS (vernacular for let's) and a host of others. These were the boys from the end of the bridge who would be my mentors.

All of the following stories are true or mostly true, depicting life in a small town in rural West Virginia from circa 1940 through 1953. They were directly or indirectly influenced by the tales from the end of the bridge, the world of my youth—long before Elvis, before the satellite dish became the West Virginia state tree, and before the mobile homes dotted the mountain sides, giving the look of an ancient Indian civilization—a world where the newest inventions were the automobile, the coal driven railroad engines and the No. 2 pencil.

Welcome to that world, which was neither round nor flat. It was Alderson, West Virginia—*my* world.

THE BARBERSHOP

At the age of eleven I was called to my father's bedside, confused by my mother's tears and the fact that my father was in bed during the middle of the day. Other than the grey tone of his skin and the glaze in his eyes, my father appeared perfectly normal. He looked at me with a faint smile, told me he was dying, handed me his pocket watch and turned his head ever so slightly to squeeze in his last breath of air.

During his lifetime, my father was a simple man. His wardrobe consisted of two pair of blue serge wool pants, six white Arrow dress shirts (generally worn with the sleeves rolled to the elbow), an unobtrusive black leather belt, two pair of black cap-toed lace up dress boots with the tops just above the ankle and his white gold Illinois railroad watch, which he wound once every day, usually in the morning. He had a blue cardigan sweater for winter, a blue serge suit coat for funerals and two dark colored ties, also for funerals. He had a pair of dime store glasses for reading and upper and lower false teeth, occasionally worn for special events, rarely for eating.

My father was a hulk of a man, standing more than six feet tall, at a time when most men were much shorter, and weighing at one time more than two hundred fifty pounds. But, I never knew that man. Illness had taken its toll before my age of recollection. All of his teeth were pulled, ostensibly as a cure for the illness, and his bulk diminished from year to year until his death, when he weighed about one hundred fifty pounds. His face was sallow, made more so by his refusal to wear false teeth. At the last, he had sort of a prison pallor. During the last few years of his life, my father's illness was finally diagnosed as diabetes with accompanying heart disease, which ultimately caused his death.

We lived in a small railroad town nestled between the mountains in rural West Virginia, some thirty-five miles from the coal mines on one side and forty miles from the logging camps on the other. A river snaked its way through the center of town. The city hall, jail, post office, movie house, three or four beer joints, railroad station and a smattering of other businesses marked the "business" side of town. The "residential" side of town was on the other side of the river. The two sides of town were connected by a wonderful old concrete bridge with a sidewalk on both sides separated by a roadway barely wide enough for two approaching cars to pass.

I lived on the "business" side of town, in the upstairs of an old house converted into a restaurant owned and operated by my mother and father, with the help of my sister. The restaurant was centered between the Presbyterian Church and City Hall, which also housed the city jail and a general meeting room used for various governmental functions.

During the winter months, I was incarcerated in the upstairs living area, particularly during the lunch and dinner hours, threatened with all sorts of bodily harm, if lunch or dinner were somehow interrupted by noise, or God forbid, my presence. But, in the spring, summer and early fall, even at a relatively early age, the entire "business" part of town was my playground. I made my daily rounds, chatting with the policeman, the undertaker, the banker, the postmen, the grocer and even those in jail through the open, barred windows. The prisoners were my favorite. Most were drunks or prostitutes. To me, however, the faceless voices were bank robbers and killers.

So, I was quite familiar with the "business" section of town when, at the age of five, my father first took me with him to the barbershop. My sister had always cut my hair. It, therefore, came as some surprise when my father took my hand and told me that it was time I went to the barbershop. Oh, I knew something about the barbershop at a much earlier age. In my daily travels I regularly passed the barbershop, but for some inexplicable reason, I never went inside.

In retrospect, I think I must have considered the barbershop off limits—maybe because my father would leave every day except Sunday for an hour or two, after announcing, with a certain air of pride, that he was going to the barbershop. He always returned smelling of a mixture of bay rum and talcum powder, with his face, as he would say, "smoother than a baby's butt." Sometimes, I noticed that his hair had been trimmed; at other times, his shoes looked like black mirrors.

A metamorphosis took place every time my father went to the barbershop. It wasn't just the shave or the haircut or the shoe shine. My father's face seemed brighter. There was an arrogance in his walk, and a renewed assurance in his talk. Indeed, with his barbershop therapy, my father became a new man.

I later discovered that meeting with his friends was more important to my father than the services he received at the barbershop. In 1940, for those who had survived the devastation of the "great depression", those who had worked for fifty cents or less a day (when work was available), those who were aware of what it was like to be hungry, unemployed and without heat or proper clothing, true happiness involved a close bond with family and friends, those with a commonality of experiences and interests—essentially the same things we search for today but rarely find.

As we made our way to the barbershop my father gave me my instructions, "Keep quiet and listen. You may learn something. And, wait for the barber with the bad haircut." According to my father, you could always determine the skill of the barber by looking at the haircut of the individual barber. Actually, It was simple. Since each barber cut the other's hair, the barber with the bad haircut was the best barber. There were never more than two barbers in town; therefore, my father's analogy seemed more than reasonable. Even today, I favor the barber with the bad haircut.

Maybe it was my age or the fact that I was walking hand in hand with my father or maybe it was the new experience, but I felt like I was in a strange, new, wonderful world as I entered the barbershop.

We were greeted by two barbers, one cutting hair and the other shaving a man with a straight razor, and seven or eight men sitting in straight backed chairs, directly in front of the barber stations, appearing as though they were watching a great performance. "There's the Irishman and he has the Little Irishman with him," one said. Everyone else had a similar greeting before we took our place in the audience. I sat in silence, pondering my new name with a certain pride.

During my first barbershop experience, there were news reports, weather reports, discussions about politics and religion, jokes and wild stories, obviously embellished with time. A somber discussion would turn into laughter at the wink of an eye. A man sitting in one of the barber's chair told a story about one of the men in town called Crow. Crow apparently got his name from his preference for Old Crow whiskey. As the story goes, Crow returned home at about midnight one Saturday night after having a few drinks with his friends to find his wife, Hattie, on her knees praying. "Dear God," she prayed, "Please forgive my poor drunk husband." Crow stopped her, saying, "My heavens and hell Hattie, don't tell Him I'm drunk. Just tell Him I'm sick."

Each of my later visits were similar but quite different, and, each visit became a new experience, although I almost always remained a little reserved. After all, this was my father's place.

After my father's death, things changed. Oh, everyone at the barbershop was friendly, but there was an obvious sadness, particularly in the eyes. And, strange as it may seem, I cannot recall ever being referred to as "the Little Irishman" after my father's death.

It was much later when I discovered the true relationship between my father and the barbershop. My father's general appearance and the vanity associated with a clean shave, haircut and shoe shine were diametrically opposed. Then, it dawned on me. My father didn't go to the barbershop for the shave or the haircut or the shoe shine. He went to the barbershop for friendship. The barbershop was my father's escape from life's burdens. It was his haven—his *Club*, if you will.

Since leaving that small town I have searched for a barbershop like my father's barbershop, without success. Barbers became stylists, with strange names—Rickay, Jackay, Antonay—creating hair styles with stranger names and selling hair products with unpronounceable names. Barbershops became salons, with names apparently created during an LSD experience. Conversations revolve around the latest tabloids or the Soaps or maybe the best way to clip your poodle.

Currently, it is much easier to schedule open heart surgery than to schedule a salon appointment. The reception room often resembles the reception area of a classy bordello. And, like the bordello, the inner rooms consist of sparsely furnished cubicles or areas for haircutting, tanning, waxing or a host of other services directed at restoring youth or creating beauty. No longer can you select the stylist with the bad haircut. Most have bad haircuts or hair designs, as they are now called. These hair emporiums bear no resemblance to my father's barbershop.

Every few years, during a period of nostalgia, I wander back to my old hometown. I am almost always saddened. Most of the old buildings are in disrepair. Some are vacant, with boards covering the windows and doors. Other buildings have been torn down, giving the main street a snaggle-toothed look. But more disillusioning is the absence of many of the old businesses—the bank, the grocery, the theater, the beer joints, and yes, the barbershop.

Before leaving, I always managed to trace the steps of my childhood. As I passed the old building which was once my father's barbershop, I could sometimes smell the pungent odor of bay rum and talcum powder, which was impossible since the old barbershop has been closed for more than thirty years. Almost forgotten memories, memories of my time with the Irishman, always rushed through my head, leaving me with thoughts of what might have been, until the sounds of the night and the shadows of deteriorated buildings shocked me back to reality.

On one such visit, as I was walking past the old barbershop, the summer calm was broken by a soft, cool breeze. As the gentle wind swirled around me, I could swear I heard familiar voices. "Hey, there's the Little Irishman, all growed up. Where you been?"

I immediately thought about all of the places I had been and all of the wonders I had seen since leaving the little mountain town —the beauty of the sunset mirrored on the desert sand, the magic of the ocean, the hustle and bustle and the strange sounds of large cities, and much more—none of which would have impressed my old friends. Finally, a tear emerged as a small voice inside me whispered, "I haven't been anywhere special. Actually, the best part of me has been right here with you all these years... Tell the Irishman I miss him."

Then, the voice of an old friend said, "He knows."

WHEN THE FROG
GOT HIS WINGS

By their fruits ye shall know them.
Matthew 7:20

With all of the innocence of a six year old, I asked, "Bob, are you prejudiced?" Never looking up, Bob replied, "Everybody's prejudiced—colored, white, men, women—everybody." Not to be disregarded that easily, I continued, "Well, what are you prejudiced against?" "Sin," he said, as he shined his customer's shoes to a mirror finish. Somehow, I sensed that our conversation was finished. "Bob must be weary," I thought, "and when Bob was weary, he didn't want to talk—not to me, not to anyone."

No matter. My attention had already been diverted to the popping sounds of the razor strap as the barber sharpened his razor to a fine edge. The broad smile on the barber's face clearly said, "Bob got the best of you again."

I ignored the stupid barber and returned my attention to Bob. Looking up at his customer who had just handed him a half dollar and turned to walk away, Bob said, "Too much. The tip's got to relate to the price." The price for a shoe shine was fifteen cents. Bob handed the bewildered customer a quarter and thanked him for his business.

My conversations with Bob Watkins continued with some regularity over the next several years. During those years, Bob became my friend, my confidant and my teacher—quite different from our first meeting.

My first trip to the barbershop, sometime near my fifth birthday, was a total disaster. The fear associated with my first haircut was more than enough to unnerve me. Then I saw Bob. I burst into tears and was about to run from the barbershop, when a soft, deep voice summoned me to the shoeshine chair. I looked slightly upward into the most radiant face I had ever seen. The sparkling eyes and toothy grin, beaming from the coal black face erased all of my fears.

Instinctively, I was drawn to Bob despite his appearance. His ebony face, with the large indentation in the forehead, always glistened. His short legs didn't match his upper body, giving the appearance of a man on the legs of a child. But, his feet, those huge feet encased in giant black shoes, turned backward, were more than I could comprehend. And, when he sat back in a resting position on the tops of the shoes, Bob looked forever like a giant frog, ready to leap at any moment.

I later learned that both of Bob's feet had been amputated, just above the ankle, in a railroad accident, the same accident that left the ugly indentation in his forehead. It then became clear. Bob's feet were not backward; he had no feet. He stood and even walked on his knees and lower legs, covered with the large, cushioned black leather shoes, giving the appearance of abnormally large feet turned backward.

From time to time I tried walking on my knees and lower legs, but after a few minutes, the pain was unbearable. I then realized that Bob must have been in severe pain, each day of his life, from the time of the accident to the day of his death. It occurred to me that Bob spent his days quoting scripture and praising God, the same God who allowed the accident, the pain and the suffering. I was even more perplexed. Evidently, Bob sensed my confusion, for one day, when the barbershop was empty, Bob motioned for me to sit in the shoeshine chair. There, he described the railroad accident and his hospital recovery in detail. Bob said that he had been a bitter young man, unhappy with life and seemingly unable to change his destiny. He claimed that he had been a drunkard, a gambler, a womanizer and a whoremonger. I didn't know what a womanizer and a whoremonger were, but I guessed that they must have been pretty bad, being listed with drunkard and gambler, which were familiar terms, even at my early age.

Bob explained that he had spent the night with another man's wife, leaving during the early morning hours before her husband arrived, drunk, without money and totally disgusted with himself. As he attempted to board a freight train for the short ride to the railroad station, he lost his footing on the side ladder of the railroad car, and fell to the tracks below. A few minutes of excruciating pain were followed by total darkness.

A week or so later, Bob regained consciousness in a hospital bed, without feet. Bandages covered the ugly indentation in his forehead and the cuts and severe abrasions on the trunk of his body. He was at the point of death, with no will to live, cursing God and everyone around him. After a time, as he regained strength, he noticed a Bible on the bedside table. For some inexplicable reason, Bob spent days looking at the Bible. Then, one day he noticed that the Bible was open. His curiosity aroused, Bob picked up the Bible and began reading about a man called Job. He was intrigued by Job, and later by other men of the Bible, who had endured great hardships, yet remained faithful to God. Bob could relate to these men, at least to the hardships.

His reading was slow, lingering a moment on each word. Later, he would buy a dictionary, and much later Biblical reference books, but for his long hospital stay, Bob was content with reading slowly. Sometimes he read all day and well into the night. In his condition —at this point in his life, time meant nothing. He had, so to speak, nowhere to run.

Ultimately, Bob Watkins' life was transformed from drunkard, gambler, womanizer and whoremonger to servant of God, and with this transformation came a radiance or glow which masked the ugliness of his injuries, together with an uncanny understanding of the Bible and of life itself. He blamed his accident and injuries, not on God, but on his sinful ways and claimed, without reservation, that the accident was his blessing, for from that accident, Bob had found God, and with God at his side, a life with fullness and meaning.

Bob came to regard every day as Sunday. He was always dressed in a black, vested suit with a white shirt and black tie, claiming that he was forever in God's presence, which required him to look his best and to be his best.

At the close of each business day, Bob could be seen struggling to slide his heavy shoes, one in front of the other, down the main street of town, on the long journey to his furnished room in an old, deteriorating home a half mile from the barbershop, stopping every so often to look toward the surrounding mountains, particularly Keeny's Knob, the highest and most majestic of all of the mountains surrounding this quiet, rural valley town. According to Bob, "God's everywhere, but he likes the mountains best—that's where he gave Moses the ten commandments and allowed him to see the Promised Land—that's where Noah's Ark landed. Most of the great events of the Bible happened on a mountain or at the foot of a mountain."

Bob rarely walked or shuffled more than a block from the barbershop. Passing motorists, often by design, almost always stopped to give Bob a ride home or to work, and on Sundays, to church. And, it didn't make much difference which church he attended, as long as God was inside and God's people filled the pews. To no one's surprise, Bob was made welcome in every church in Town—black *and* white.

Nevertheless, Bob was somewhat partial to one of the white churches. The pastor of that church could be seen huddled with Bob on a regular basis in a corner of the barbershop deep in private conversation. The barber invariably laughed and whispered to his customer, "The preacher's getting his sermon for next Sunday."

Of all of the people I have known in this life, Bob Watkins was the only person totally without color—loved and respected by everyone he met, regardless of race, color or religion. Even the worst of sinners were welcomed by Bob with love and kindness. Bob reasoned that he was commissioned to do that which Jesus would have done, which included love and kindness toward the most despicable of mankind.

To me, Bob Watkins was without fault, except, maybe, for the times he claimed he was "weary" and didn't want to talk. During those times, he seemed to be almost in a trance, his mind being transfixed on someone, or something, or someplace far away. My father said that Bob knew so much about Heaven, he was forever homesick.

Sometime before midnight on a clear Summer night, Bob Watkins was called home by his Heavenly Father. He was found the next morning by his landlady, slumped in his dilapidated easy chair, with a smile on his face, and his old, tattered Bible opened in his lap to the book of Acts. A part of Acts 7:55 was underlined, which read, "...looked up to heaven and saw the glory of God, and Jesus standing at the right hand of God."

On the floor, beside the easy chair was a small white feather. The doctor and the men from the funeral home looked at the feather and agreed that it probably came from the bed ticking. The old landlady, however, knew better. The bed was still made up like she had left it that morning, and she had never before seen feathers on the floor. The old woman knew in her heart, without any doubt whatsoever —the old frog finally got his wings.

THE RACE THAT NEVER WAS

There must have been fifteen or twenty young men gathered at the end of the bridge, telling tall tales, for want of anything better to do, on a warm Saturday in July. Some, generally the elders, were sitting on the ramp or walkway of a billboard sign, constructed by the sign company for installing new billboard signs and used by the boys at the end of the bridge, alternatively as a stage or as a seating area. Everyone else was standing, facing the sign or turned in one direction or another to watch the young women and teen age girls crossing the bridge or making an entrance or exit from Mack's Snack Shack, which was also a gathering place for young people of both sexes, located some twenty feet west of the billboard sign—within earshot of the signboard, but a respectable distance from the boys at the end of the bridge.

Life in the '50s was a strange mixture of the Victorian and the vulgar, and there was no better display of those opposite cultures than at the end of the bridge. Men, especially those who were married or attached, either crossing the bridge or making their entrance or exit from Mack's Snack Shack, would give a longing look toward the boys at the end of the bridge, while the women, young and old, would look the other way, as though the boys and the signboard simply did not exist.

The local police force, consisting of two rather inept police officers who generally traveled as a pair in the city's single police car, was frequently the topic of conversation. The officers, nicknamed Pepsi and Pete (for some reason I cannot remember), gave the appearance of authority; however, when trouble occurred, real trouble involving violence, both Pepsi and Pete were almost always keeping the peace on the other side of town. Someone said that Pete was like a man with one leg in an ass kicking contest and that Pepsi wasn't much better.

At the end of the bridge, one of the boys was reciting a story about Pepsi stopping an out of state motorist for speeding. As the story goes, Pepsi pulled over the motorist, got out of the police car and walked with an authoritative swagger to the "subject's" car. Using his best police techniques Pepsi asked, in his deep voice, "Boy, where you from?" The subject replied that he was from Chicago, after which Pepsi again asked, "Then what the hell are you doing with those Illinois plates on your car?" The story was acted out by the story teller and offered as "the God's honest truth", a phrase which accompanied most tales at the end of the bridge.

Suddenly, a car nearby backfired. Everyone was startled, because the sound was much like the sound of a shotgun discharged at close range. Then, there was the sound of squealing and the roar of an engine, a signal that Mocas had arrived.

Mocas was, for lack of better words, an automotive savant. He knew every part of every car or truck, could efficiently repair most defects (sometimes with a hair pin or chewing gum) and had made or fabricated parts for his old car, a beat up old Ford named "Eight Ball", which, if not "Mocas rigged", would have been junked years before. Eight Ball was parked next to a gas pump at the ESSO service station, which had closed an hour before, directly across the highway from the sign board.

Everyone at the end of the bridge waited to see whether Mocas would join us at the sign board or would walk to the pool room owned and managed by his parents, which was located on the other side of the bridge. As a general rule, if Mocas walked toward the pool room, everyone would remain at the sign board, but if Mocas joined us at the end of the bridge, everyone, singularly or in groups of two or three, would gravitate toward the pool room, as a means of escaping his incessant lecture on the subject of car parts.

The pool room was actually a beer joint with three pool tables and with bootleg whiskey openly sold by the pint, with little regard for the proximity of Pepsi or Pete. Throughout the evening hours, Mocas' father would yell, irrespective of those present, "Rack the balls Alice, while I get the boys another pint of M & M." It followed that Mocas' mother was referred to by the boys at the end of the bridge as "Rack the Balls Alice".

This night, Mocas walked toward the sign board, which everyone believed would mark the beginning of a mass exodus to the pool room. At about the same time, we saw Don Bryant parking his new 1952 Buick Skylark convertible in front of Mack's Snack Shack. This was, without a doubt, the most beautiful car I had every seen. It had a red leather interior, a black top, wire wheels with wide white side wall tires (sometimes called gangster walls) and all of the accessories available at that time. This was one of only five hundred manufactured by the Buick Motor Company. Everyone at the end of the bridge surrounded the Buick before Don could open the driver's door.

Now, Don Bryant was not one of the boys at the end of the bridge. He was in his mid thirties and married with a beautiful blond infant daughter named Patty. Moreover, Don had a good job with the West Virginia Highway Department, which automatically precluded him from unofficial membership of the boys at the end of the bridge. Besides, Don was not prone to foul language, a factor which definitely kept him from the end of the bridge.

Within a minute or so, Mocas had pushed his way through the crowd, moving up next to the driver's side door where he blurted, "That's a damn nice looking car, but it's a little light under the hood."

I could see Don's face getting red from the neck up. Then, Don said, "Well, Mocas, it has a V8 engine; the biggest engine Buick puts in a car."

"That may be, but it can't hold a candle to old Eight Ball over there," Mocas replied.

Everyone laughed, including Don, which made Mocas furious.

Mocas began to taunt Don and demand a race of the cars from the edge of town to Fort Spring, a distance of about six miles. I think Don must have regressed to a time when he was younger and wilder, because after about ten minutes of listening to the taunting and cursing of Mocas, Don said, "O.K. Mocas, we'll race to Fort Spring."

Mocas ran across the street, jumped into the driver's seat of Eight Ball and began to crank the engine. There was a grinding noise, but the engine would not start. Finally, Mocas yelled from the open window, "Don, drive over here and give old Eight Ball a push so we can get started."

With a smile on his face, Don started the Buick, pressed down on the accelerator so that Mocas could appreciate the full power of the engine, and drove past Mocas and Eight Ball on his way home, slightly spinning the rear wheels of the Buick for effect. Thus ended the race that never was.

THE CHIEF

Richard Ford and Marguerite Rowe stood on either side of one of the large tables, quickly and quietly separating a montage of letters, packages, newspapers and advertisements, poured from the faded green bags, marked "U.S. Mail," just delivered to the Alderson Post Office from the C&O Railway Station, located across Railroad Avenue. The bare concrete floor beneath their feet was discolored and marred from the constant shuffling of feet over the years. They were postmen, those who had inherited, by employment, the principles of the U.S. Postal Service which had existed for more than a century—principles that dictated an unusual discipline and dedication to the identification, distribution and delivery of mail, promptly and properly. And, none were better at their job than Richard and Marguerite.

Together, they knew everyone within a thirty mile radius of the post office, knew most of their family members, what they did for a living and sometimes a secret or two from the handwriting or smell of an envelope or package. Richard, in particular, could read the most unintelligible hand writing and prided himself on identifying each piece of mail within a maximum time of two days, sometimes delivering the mail to the addressee himself.

Richard was rather austere—maybe stoic is a better word. In any case, there was little room for laughter in his life. The Postmaster, Duncan Johnson, on each performance report, described Richard as determined and dedicated.

This day was like most others. The quick eyes and deft fingers sorted the mail for the post office boxes and sent the mail carriers on their several routes. Then, suddenly, the shrill sound of the siren,

atop the old Woodson & Prince Wholesale Grocery building, a block
from the Post Office, summoned the men of the Alderson Volunteer
Fire Department.

Richard, without hesitation, dropped the mail in his hands,
sprinted from the rear of the building and down an alley to the City
Hall, opened the garage door to the stall that housed the old fire
engine, a vintage late '20s or early '30s A-Model Ford, customized
to carry the necessary fire fighting equipment. Charlie Lobban,
proprietor of Lobban's Funeral Home directly across the street from
City Hall gave Richard the needed information on the location of
the fire, between his intermittent coughs, which were a trademark,
then ran to his ambulance to follow the fire truck—just in case there
was someone injured, or maybe dead.

Richard drove the ancient fire truck from it's bay to the center
of South Monroe Street and waited for the other volunteer firemen,
running from all directions. The adrenalin rushing through his body,
his rising blood pressure and the sounds from the sirens changed
his personality. He was alive again. He was Chief of the Alderson
Volunteer Fire Department—at this moment in time, the most
important man in Alderson, West Virginia.

This scene was reenacted, time and time again, throughout the
years. Richard Ford earned his living as a postman; yet he was only
alive, really alive, in his role as The Chief.

Richard's off days, vacation days and holidays were usually spent
at the fire hall, cleaning, waxing, folding the hoses, tuning the engine
of the old fire truck, reading about the latest fire fighting methods
or just hanging out, waiting for the next sound of the siren. He used
a part of his income from the City to purchase new equipment
or to satisfy some other need of the fire department. The Mayor
always used the terms "determined" and "dedicated" to describe the
Chief.

As the Chief, Richard assumed other city duties. For example,
he assisted the city's policeman or policemen (sometimes there were
two), especially during Halloween, removing lawn furniture and

other property from the railroad tracks, just prior to the destruction of the property by collision with a passing train. The culprits who lay in the weeds to wait the train wreck, always escaped in the darkness, and the lawn furniture and other property was later delivered to the owners. Richard likely knew the names of those involved; however, no suspects were ever identified.

In fact, Richard knew the names of those who turned over the outhouses, stole the watermelons and rode down the fodder shocks in the fields, but he never disclosed a single name. He even knew about the Halloween night that Lonnie Shires and a couple of friends were turning over an outhouse near the First Baptist Church, when Lonnie fell head first into the murky hole. He looked terrible, like some prehistoric monster, and he smelled worse. Lonnie ran to the river bank, discarded all of his clothing, and jumped into the cold waters of the Greenbrier River. He remained in the water for the longest time, while one of his friends ran home and retrieved clean clothing, a towel and a pair of oversized boots. Richard knew the entire story but kept silent.

In my teens, sometimes suffering from extreme boredom, especially during the summer months, I would stop by city hall and help Richard—cleaning the fire engine, cleaning and polishing the fire axes, folding hoses and doing other tasks, as directed by the Chief. One day when I was 17, or thereabouts, Richard said, "How would you like to be an apprentice fireman. At first, you would be an observer. Then, you could assist with the hoses, and in two or three years you would fight fire with the seasoned firemen. Besides, it pays five dollars for each fire call." I was ecstatic.

It was a little more than three weeks, at exactly 11:07 p.m. on a Saturday, before the siren announced the next fire. I had just returned home from the end of the bridge. Like Richard, I felt the adrenalin rush, as I put on the old clothes set aside for fighting fires and ran to the fire station next door.

The Chief had already pulled the engine from the bay, into the middle of the street, and had already received notice of the location of the fire from the funeral director, when I jumped on the running board of the old fire engine. I was the first to arrive, besides Richard and Charlie. "I am finally a firefighter," I thought, as we waited for my fellow firefighters, running toward the truck.

To my surprise, I saw Wire and Axe Head headed toward the fire truck in a running stagger. As they got closer, it was apparent that they had just come from one of the beer joints nearby. I couldn't understand why Wire or Axe Head would be welcomed by the Chief. Then, it dawned on me that this was a volunteer fire department and that I was probably the only one on the truck who had been invited by the Chief.

Men were still jumping onto the fire truck as the old truck sputtered and gasped, moving across the railroad tracks, the bridge and up the hill toward the burning house. As we approached the house, I could see flames from an upstairs window, followed by the billowing smoke. A crowd had already gathered at the front of the house, as the Chief began issuing orders. I was assigned to help with one of the hoses.

One of the men immediately removed a fire axe from the side of the truck, ran to the front door and began to chop on the door, when out of the crowd a voice yelled, "No, you dumb s.o.b. The door's unlocked." The energetic fireman stopped chopping and turned the door knob. The door opened. Some shook their head in total dismay. Others simply laughed.

As the front door opened, Wire and Axe Head rushed into the house. At first, I had been skeptical, but seeing the dynamic duo enter the house, with the fire still blazing, totally without fear, I was impressed.

Richard was giving instructions about using safety, when one of the firemen yelled, "Richard, come quick." Richard ran to the fireman, and after a short conversation, the Chief scurried up a ladder toward the belching fire, without his safety belt, used to remain on the ladder and direct the hose. When the Chief turned on the hose, the water pressure of the hose literally threw him backward and off the ladder. Richard fell to the ground, breaking a bone in his left arm. Someone put a sling on his left arm, but Richard, in obvious pain remained at the fire, giving orders to everyone within the sound of his voice, until the fire was finally extinguished.

I rode back to City Hall with Richard and two or three others. Most just walked home, fatigued after a night's work. I commented, to no one in particular, that I had not seen Wire or Axe Head after I saw them running into the house. Richard didn't seem concerned. In fact, he almost smiled.

The following night, at the end of the bridge, the subject was the big fire. By general consensus if your house caught on fire in Alderson, West Virginia you had two choices: you could watch the house burn to the ground; or, you could have it chopped down by the Alderson Volunteer Fire Department.

I then discovered what happened to Wire and Axe Head. Someone reported that after rushing into the house they found the location of the whiskey cabinet, emptied all of the liquor they could carry and ran out the back door toward the river bank. Supposedly, they were still passed out on the river bank, somewhere between Markley's Pool and Camp Greenbrier, with sufficient whiskey for at least two more days.

I never responded to another fire call. At 17, I didn't have the determination or dedication to be a fireman.

THE LITTLE GERMAN

September 8, 1942, was one of the most memorable days of my life. It was the first day of my second grade class at Alderson Elementary School. I felt quite comfortable, much different from my first year. This year, I knew everyone in class, including the teacher, most of the upperclassmen and every inch of the small school building, including the immediate playground and the adjoining athletic field, sometimes used by the elementary school for recess, but in reality dedicated for the use of the high school football team, the pride of my hometown.

The past nine months had been a blur. On December 7, 1941, the Japanese attacked Pearl Harbor, a name not in my vocabulary and a place I couldn't envision. During the months that followed, a cold wind blew through the valley, taking with it all of the able bodied young men, leaving behind the old men, women and children —the fathers, mothers, brothers and sisters of those who had been taken to fight and sometimes shed their blood or die on islands of the south pacific or the beaches of Europe, or in the alternative, those who left town to work twelve hour shifts in the shipyards or factories, making the ships, tanks, jeeps, armaments, clothing and other goods necessary for war. War was declared, first on Japan, then Germany. Our government implemented rationing of sugar, gasoline and a myriad of other products. And, the faces of those left behind—those faces which had shown such happiness and contentment—now reflected fear, anxiety, sadness and uncertainty. In the dark months of the war, I, like most of those in my town, learned to hate both Germans and Japanese equally. As the days passed, I played "army" with my friends, fighting an invisible enemy, sometimes Japs, more often Germans, since none of us were willing to play the part of a hated enemy.

The second grade class at school was finally called to order by our teacher, Miss Evelyn Warren, who announced that we had a new student in class and summoned him to the front of the room to tell the class something about himself. The toe headed boy with the golden tan and sky blue eyes walked to the front of the room, turned to face the class and said, "I'm Howard James Rowe, III. They call me Jimmy. My father is Jim Rowe. He works at the women's prison. My grandfather, H.J. Rowe, is sometimes called Howard. He lives across the road from the river and sells coal and brick. We moved here this summer from Narrows, Virginia, and I'm a German."

The class was totally silent. Even Miss Warren was speechless. Finally, she began speaking in a nervous monotone, but I heard nothing. The only thing on my mind was the revelation that Jimmy Rowe was a German. He said so himself. I was stunned.

The word rapidly spread that we had a confessed German in our school. For the next several weeks, Jimmy Rowe was engaged in a verbal or physical fight during recess or after school on a daily basis.

I was devastated. In June, Jimmy and his family moved into a rental house across the street and two doors south of my home. We became friends, playing together every day, from morning until after dark—even played "army"—and nothing was ever said or done to indicate that I was in the company of a confessed German—maybe an enemy agent, perhaps a spy.

After school, I found my daddy in the back yard, sitting in his old wooden garden chair. Speaking softly, so that my mother couldn't hear, I said, "Today, Jimmy Rowe stood up in front of the whole class and said he was a German. He might even be some sort of enemy agent." Daddy smiled, and without hesitation, replied, "That's old man H.J. talking—not Jimmy. The family probably did come from Germany a couple of generations ago, but the Rowe family is as American as you and me. Our ancestors came from Ireland, which makes you and me Irish. Yet, we're all American." I was satisfied and relieved that my friend was a German, but not really a "German."

A few years later, I was invited to accompany Jimmy on a Sunday ride with his grandfather, whom I had never seen. The black Packard was shined to perfection. The old man, Jimmy and I occupied the back seat, while the old man's driver was alone in the front seat. After giving instructions to his driver, H.J. sat back to enjoy his afternoon ride.

When I first saw Jimmy's grandfather, I immediately recalled my father's words, "That's old man H.J. talking...." A smile must have crossed my face as I surveyed the old German. He was a wiry man, maybe 4' 9" tall, or thereabouts. The deep tan of his hands and bald head, showing from his black three piece suit, heavily starched white shirt and black tie centered by an unusual tie pin, attested to the time spent outdoors. He reminded me of a German General on a Sunday drive in the country. "It's possible that he is a German spy," I thought. Again, I remembered my father's words, "We're all Americans," and dismissed thoughts of spies and espionage

On this trip, H.J. was very solemn, viewing the countryside and the houses, commenting, from time to time, on the names of those living there, or those who used to live there, and every so often, telling the driver, "Show him your ass," instructions to pass the car in front.

Jimmy related a story about H.J. concerning the purchase of a truck from a Pentecostal preacher as evidence of the old man's business ability. The preacher said to Mr. Rowe, "I have talked to the Lord about the sale of this here truck, and the Lord told me I should get $1,000.00 for the truck."

Unperplexed by the preacher's statement, H.J. replied, "You get your ass over there under the tree and talk to the Lord again. Tell him I'm not going to give you a dime more than $600.00 for that truck. The preacher walked over to the tree, knelt on his knees for several minutes. Thereafter, he raised himself and returned to confront Mr. Rowe. With a smile on his face, the preacher said, "The Lord said that $600.00 wasn't a bad deal. The sale of the truck was then finalized to the satisfaction of both parties and the blessing of the Lord.

In the weeks that followed the first day of school, Jimmy slowly became Jimmy the American. He acquired a large, yellow mongrel dog and named him G.I. Joe, a sure sign of patriotism, and he never again spoke of being a German or of Germany in any endearing terms. Joe became our friend and our constant companion for the next 8-10 years.

During those weeks and for the next couple of years, Jimmy and I played football in a graveled parking lot beside my house— sometimes against each other, mostly against Grub Lobban and Sookie Clifford, both of whom were five or six years our senior. We always left the game with bruises and abrasions on almost every part of our body, torn clothing and damaged egos but vowing to get those no good "bladderskites" or those damned "shikepokes" tomorrow. We never did.

Jimmy was easily the most articulate of all of my friends, using words and phrases which were near poetic, but with immediate clarity. For example, if Jimmy said, "It's colder than a well digger's ass in January," or "Old Mike lives so far back in the woods that he has to wipe the owl shit off the clock to see what time it is," or, "That common son of a bitch is lower than whale shit and that's at the bottom of the sea," no further explanation was required.

And, even words which had no real meaning were somehow given instant meaning. "That no good bladderskite," or, "That low down shikepoke," left no doubt that Jimmy was referring to a person of unsavory character. No further explanation was necessary.

During those years, Jimmy and I became closer than brothers. Where one was seen, the other was close by. For example, when I was eleven, I broke my leg in a silly playground accident. As several men were helping me to a car to transport me for medical treatment, Jimmy ran down an alley to notify my parents. On seeing my father, Jimmy said, "Mr. Ayers, H.R. just broke his leg and he may be dead by now. They're taking him to Dr. Mahood's office."

A group of people gathered at the doctor's office, as the old doctor, who delivered me into this world, inspected my left leg. According to him, the fragmented thigh bone would require surgery and hospitalization. Dr. Mahood said, "I need two long splints to stabilize his leg so that we can get him to the hospital." Jimmy left. I wondered why Jimmy, my best friend, had left me at a time when I really needed him.

The doctor continued, stating that he didn't have any splints and didn't know where he could find any splints. Everyone was trying to figure out what could be used as substitute splints and where they could be found. During the conversations, I heard a loud commotion, then saw Jimmy running into the examining room with two long pieces of wood. I later learned that Jimmy had gone to his house, a couple of doors from Dr. Mahood's office, and with a hatchet, chopped the two splints from the siding on his house. During my three months in the hospital, I thought about my splints and my friend who dared chop siding from his house so that I could be transported to the hospital without causing further injury. This was, indeed, the act of a friend... no, much more than a friend, a very special friend.

At the age of 11, Jimmy moved to a farmhouse, next to the rear of the Women's Federal Prison, and on June 21 of that year I was invited to the Rowe home to celebrate Jimmy's 12th birthday and spend the night.

After dinner, Jimmy and I decided to play football in the massive yard that bordered a corn field. After a few plays, Jimmy stopped and exclaimed, "God, Ayers, if I break this new watch I got for my birthday, my daddy will have my ass. Here, Joe!" G.I. Joe slowly walked toward his master. Jimmy removed the gold watch with the roman numerals and leather band from his wrist and fastened the watch on one of the dog's legs. Old Joe walked over to a large tree, laid down and closed his eyes. In a few minutes, Joe got up, growled and ran toward the corn field. I saw a rabbit crossing the yard and moving between the rows of corn. Joe followed.

I thought Jimmy could cuss but I discovered that his dad was the master. Big Jim knew cuss words I had never heard and he used every cuss word he knew as we searched the lawn and the corn field for hours, with the aid of flashlights. The birthday watch was never found.

At the age of 13 Jimmy discovered chewing tobacco—first the loose tobacco, then the twist and finally his favorite, "Bull of the Woods", a plug tobacco with a slight taste of kerosene or something worse. I regularly chewed with Jimmy as an act of camaraderie but I never really liked chewing tobacco.

It was about that time that Jimmy and I began hanging out at the end of the bridge—chewing, spitting and telling tales. Both of us spent so much time at the end of the bridge that there was little time for homework. This became evident in school. We would try to use our wits rather than book knowledge to satisfy the teachers. Sometimes it worked. More often it didn't.

In Civics class, the teacher entered the room and orally stated, "Write a page or less on what you know about the Monroe Doctrine." Jimmy's paper read, "There ain't enough doctors in Greenbrier County, so those in Greenbrier County have to go to Monroe County for their doctor'n." This seemed reasonable to Jimmy since our home town was partly in Greenbrier County and partly in Monroe County and most of the doctors were located on the Monroe County side of town. Needless to say, the teacher was not impressed.

In his Junior year, Jimmy was caught again. A book report was due in English class and Jimmy had spent so much time at the end of the bridge that he had hardly opened a book much read a book. The report was due in two days and Jimmy began to panic. He went to Lute Mann's store, bought a Classic Comic book and spent the next two days writing his report. The report was well done and turned in on time. A few days later, Stella Nelson, the English teacher directed Jimmy to stay after class. She told Jimmy that his report was well written and very neat; however, she knew that Jimmy had not read the book. The book was *The Illiad* by Homer, a difficult book to read for college students much less juniors in high school. "Damn Lute Mann," said Jimmy, "He should know better than to carry Classic Comics that you can't report on. Why else would anyone buy those damned books?"

After high school and a semester of college, Jimmy's life and my life took different roads. We telephone each other a couple of times a year, and every five or six years we meet each other in Alderson, West Virginia. We talk about our families, the state of the world, the fact that the old home town just isn't the same and tell tall tales for a few hours. When leaving town, we each stop at the end of the bridge long enough to allow the memories of the past to create a tear or two. Then, we each take a different road. He to his world. Me to mine. I still miss the Little German.

By the way, if you happen to visit the old farm house on the back side of the Women's Prison and you find an old watch with a ragged leather band, close your eyes and softly rub the old, rusty watch. If you're lucky, your mind might just conger up the vision of a young boy with blond hair, blue eyes and a golden tan, walking with an old yellow dog named G.I. Joe. If you do, don't piss him off. He might just call you a no good bladderskite or a low down shikepoke or something worse. Should this occur, you have just met my friend, Howard James Rowe, III—the Little German.

LOOKING FOR
THE GREENER GRASS

Some people are quite content with their lot in life, completely happy with their life style, their talents, their jobs and all of their possessions—all of those toys each of us accumulate and discard throughout our lifetime. Many of those people consider themselves blessed by God, recognizing their own weakness and the insignificance of their own being but realizing that their achievements have been far greater than deserved. Unfortunately, I have never been one of those people. I have spent my entire life in a frenzy, frantically searching for the greener grass, only to find, as I progressed through my later years of life, that I had always stood on the greenest grass of all.

High school football was a prime example. I spent four years, and probably longer, in a love/hate relationship with football, celebrating winning season after winning season but never being fully satisfied—always looking for something better.

And, while I lived in a certain torment throughout the high school years, I never complained, especially about football, this being the macho period of my life and football, especially in my hometown, being considered something of a religious experience. The coach, Alexander Arbucle McLaughlin, known by everyone as Abe, a legend as a player at West Virginia Tech and a greater legend as a high school football coach, was, indeed, the high priest, revered by everyone, including opposing coaches and townspeople, all of whom spent an inordinate time trying to figure out the reasons for Abe's success. As a result, the football field became Holy Ground, and all of those boys turned to men who played before me—those responsible for the rows of glass encased championship trophies in the office and hallway of the high school, served as apostles, proclaiming the word—that Alderson High School did not and would not lose football games. Caught up in this atmosphere, I had no choice. Like it or not, I had to play high school football.

My freshman year was, from the very beginning, a disaster. In the late Summer of 1949, several of my classmates and friends arrived at the football locker room at least an hour before opening practice, feeling larger than life and eager to begin our quest for hero status—a status achieved instantly upon graduation, through self serving declarations, embellished with each new recollection until hero status was acknowledged by most, if not all, of the apostles.

In one hand I clutched an authorization form, with the forged signature of my mother who believed that football was, at best, nonsense. I, therefore, coaxed a neighborhood girl, whose writing was more adult than mine, into signing my mother's name. Afterward, both of us suffered guilt and fear, thinking that our crime would soon be discovered and that we would both be subjected to severe punishment—maybe even jail. Nevertheless, the fear of being chided by the boys at the end of the bridge prevailed. I was not about to be labeled as a "wuss".

In my other hand, I held a paper bag containing a new jock strap (my first) and a new pair of athletic socks. My knees were shaking. The thought of being discovered a forger was bad enough. I was now faced with the realization that I must prove myself as a football player which was far worse.

Finally, the equipment manager arrived, hurriedly gathered the authorization forms and stuffed them into a large brown envelope. I breath a sign of relief, confident that my mother's forged signature would never be discovered. Next, the manager announced that all of the incoming freshman would need to step to the back of the line while he issued uniforms, pads, shoes and helmets to the upper-classmen. This seemed more than reasonable. I knew that it would take several practice sessions before the coach would recognize my athletic talents and elevate me to at least a second string position, maybe as a wingback, but most probably as an end where I would catch virtually every pass thrown in my direction.

The upperclassmen were already dressing when the freshmen were allowed to enter the dressing room, although they looked nothing like the players I had seen on game nights. They wore old, dingy uniforms, stained, tattered and torn from hours of battle and years of wear. After the initial shock, I realized that the good uniforms, like the Sunday suit, must be kept for special occasions.

In time, the manager came out of the equipment room with my uniform. I was elated. The shoes, helmet and pads looked almost new, although the uniform itself was as worn and tattered as all of the others. The manager smiled as he handed me my uniform saying, "Wear this one with pride. It belonged to Ray Bostic." I could see the envy on the face of my friends. Seemingly, I had received special treatment. I reasoned that the coach had somehow discovered my rare athletic ability, even before the start of practice.

The irony quickly became apparent as I donned my uniform. The shoulder pads and hip pads were abnormally large. The bottom of the pants, which were supposed to fit just below the knee, were just above my ankles. The shoes were at least two sizes too large and the helmet was a size eight, a full three fourths size too large. I must have resembled some sort of clown.

It was only then that the person and the name began to mesh. Ray Bostic was probably the largest player ever to play for Alderson High School. He stood about six foot five, weighed a full two hundred forty pounds and had a head the size of a large melon. Ray was obviously the product of a flaw in genetics, for my larger teammates weighed less than one hundred eighty pounds and stood less than six feet tall.

I can understand your skepticism. Now, it is not unusual for football players, even high school players, to be much larger than Ray Bostic. I have often wondered why men, and even women, are so much bigger today than they were forty years ago. Natural evolution, of course, is one possibility. Even selective breeding another, but I have this theory, formulated after great thought and circumspection, that today's giants are a product of McDonald's hamburgers and french fries. Think about it for a moment. There were no men approaching seven feet in height and weighing more than three hundred pounds before McDonald's.

In any event, when all of the Freshmen were fully dressed, looking more like homeless waifs than football players, the equipment manager said without any emotion, "Take the field." And, take the field we did, yelling and screaming like an ancient tribe of warriors going into battle, running, as fast as we could the thirty yards or so from the locker room to the entrance to the football field, hampered by the weight of our equipment and the strange fitting uniforms.

I was in the middle of the pack, one hand firmly gripping the waist of my pants to keep them from falling and the other hand desperately trying to keep my helmet in place. The pace slowed as we reached the entrance to the field. There was a flagstone walkway between two stone ticket booths, requiring a sharp left turn for the gaggle of young warriors, most of whom were taken by surprise, although each of us was aware of the lay of the land and the flagstone walkway. Yet, none of us had ever worn shoes with cleats.

In turning left, my helmet turned right. I was partially blinded by the ear section of the helmet and did not see the flagstone walkway. The cleats of my oversized shoes skidded on the flagstone, and after several contortions, I fell with a mighty thud on the flagstone. I was addled for a moment, remembering only that firm hands were lifting and carrying me to a grass area on the sidelines. Finally in control of my faculties, with helmet removed, I immediately noticed blood soaking through the right elbow of my jersey. I also had abrasions on my right arm and both legs. These were of little consequence. The cut on my elbow, however, was a large gaping wound which should have required a number of stitches.

I stoically rejected offers for medical treatment, electing instead to be bandaged by the equipment manager. As it turned out, this was the most severe injury I received during my four years of high school football and the only time I was rendered unconscious.

Coach McLaughlin, a man of very few words, left the upperclassmen and walked to where I was sitting. He looked for a moment at the blood oozing from the gash in my elbow, then turned and walked away. I could hear him mumble, "Gosh darn boys... if they can't get onto the field without getting hurt, what kind of team are we going to have?"

I dreaded going back to the locker room after practice, keenly aware that my fall would be the subject of conversation. Instead of showering, I took a "whore bath" at one of the sinks and dressed quickly to leave before the rest of the team finished showering. As I walked past the shower room, I heard one of the boys, in a mimicking voice say, "Gosh darn boys...". I hurried out of the locker room with the laughter of thirty or more of my teammates ringing in my ears.

I walked home alone, taking a circuitous route to insure my solitude, wondering how I was going to keep my mother from seeing the bandage on my elbow. I remember thinking that this is how I would feel if the Rapture came and I was the only person left.

I entered my house like a burglar, fully expecting to be caught, but my mother was busy and I was able to change into a long sleeve shirt before anyone was aware of my presence. I continued to wear long sleeve shirts, without notice, first to hide the bandages and then to hide the ugly scar.

It was mid-season before my mother discovered that I was a member of the football team. By that time, my scar lost some of its angry look and I was settled in as a member of the football team. By osmosis, I became intoxicated with each winning game, cheering my teammates, my companions on the field of battle, with such vigor that I was almost as exhausted after the game as those who had taken the field. And, in practice I was gaining more confidence with each passing week. Yet, I dreaded the awful confrontation with my mother.

Looking from the kitchen window, and without otherwise acknowledging my presence, my mother, in a bland, emotionless voice said, "I understand you're playing football." At this point, I knew better than to lie. I replied affirmatively, ending the conversation. My mother never mentioned football again. A year later, when I was a first string tackle, my mother attended one game, left at half time and never returned. Apparently, she could not stomach the violence of the game—violence affecting her youngest child. In true character, she never discussed attending the game.

Coach McLaughlin was a simple man who spoke sparingly, often mumbling unintelligible phrases, preceded by the words "gosh darn." He never cussed or shouted or became enraged, but his eyes and his body language spoke volumes. Everyone knew when old Abe was displeased, and no one, absolutely no one, ever wanted to be the subject of that displeasure. As a result, I always tried to stay on Coach's blind side, as a kind of invisible ninja. It got to the point where I could feel his stare. In those moments, I always managed to be a step quicker and a notch more powerful than my opponent, in stark contrast to some of my teammates, who always seemed to screw up at the very time old Abe was watching.

This, together with the limited number of seniors, elevated me to starting tackle at the beginning of my sophomore year. Before the first game, I was issued a new helmet and a new pair of shoes, leaving little doubt that I would be playing with some regularity, but even before the new helmet and shoes, I knew that I would be a starter in the first game of the season, a disclosure made by two graduates at the end of the bridge, following the first contact scrimmage of the season. The boys at the end of the bridge were rarely wrong about such things.

For the next two years, I started at both offensive tackle and defensive tackle. However, I spent at least half of each practice session at offensive end and defensive end. I detested the tackle position, where I was sure to be confronted by the meanest, biggest man on the opposing team, but I loved playing end—both offensively and defensively. As an offensive end, I was an eligible receiver on passing plays and as a defensive end, I could sometimes create havoc in the opponent's backfield. I was well suited to playing end. I was agile and I could catch a pass better than anyone on the team. Besides, ends often wind up as heros. No tackle has ever been considered a hero, except maybe to a running back.

During those two years, the regular end was a year my senior, accompanied by game experience. Much as it hurt, I was content with my fate, knowing that I would be playing end during my senior year. And so I continued, biding my time, practicing part time at end and playing each game at tackle.

Then, my senior year rolled around, and sure enough, I began practice at end. The first scrimmage was a disaster. The new tackle couldn't block on passing plays and the passer was sacked on every passing play by the defensive end before any of the receivers could get into a pass route.

The next two scrimmages were repetitions of the first. Finally, Coach told me to switch back to tackle, moving the new tackle to end. At first I was mortified, then elated when the new end dropped the first five or six passes thrown to him. It can't be long, I thought, before old Abe switches me back to end.

This didn't happen. Game after game, I blocked the opposing defensive end well out of reach of our passer, and throughout the season, no passes were ever thrown to the new end. During that time, I harbored a great deal of resentment. Later, I realized that Coach Abe made the only rational decision for the survival of the team.

So, I ended my high school football career wearing a school letter with a football, three bars for the number of years lettered and a star, designating co-captain—in pseudo-contentment that each of those years had been winning years but disappointed by the realization that in those three years I had only touched a football a half dozen times on blocked punts and fumble recoveries. Only once, on a blocked punt and return for a touchdown, did I ever feel the joy of crossing the goal line and raising my arms in victory. Nevertheless, I reasoned that it was better to be a journeyman on a winning team than a hero on a losing team.

Years later, I followed my son's football career, through junior-pro, junior high and high school, as he emerged in high school as a running back with unusual quickness and speed and the ability to cut back against the grain like a cat—smooth and agile with every move—traits obviously inherited from his mother. During those years, Chris did all of those things I wanted to do in high school and more, setting new records for his high school team, a few of which remain unbroken. With each touchdown, he simply hung his head and walked to the sidelines, delayed by the cheers and hugs of his teammates—not pompous and belligerent like I would have been.

One fall Saturday afternoon, my son and I were lounging in our den, watching a televised college game. He was nursing his football wounds from the night before. I was simply bonding with my son, or at least that was my intention. From raising an older daughter, I had learned that teenagers, male or female, were erratic creatures, who harbored a deep distrust for the adult world. To them, any meaningful conversation should be avoided at all costs.

At halftime, I cautiously started my meaningful conversation with Chris. Well, at least the conversation was meaningful from my perspective. I told Chris of my pride in seeing him play football. I spoke of his accomplishments, his running ability, his winning attitude and much more. I told Chris all of those feelings I had kept inside me for the past three or four years.

Chris' response was totally unexpected. "Dad," he said. "You don't really understand. Sometimes, I am running for my life. It's no fun to be hit by two or three guys who weigh from two hundred to two hundred fifty pounds."

I was shocked. I always thought he liked being a running back. "Are you saying that you don't like football?" I replied.

He sort of hung his head. "Sometimes," he said, then continued, "Yes, sometimes I don't like football. But mostly, I think it's more fun to hit than to be hit. I'd just like to play defense, a defensive back or a linebacker, where I could hit someone else for a change."

Indeed, for the first time, I discovered a bond between my son and I. We were, unfortunately, both in search of the greener grass, so much so that we failed to look at the grass beneath our very feet.

Perhaps my grandson will play end or defensive back or linebacker, or maybe he will play golf or music or play nothing at all. As he grows to maturity, my ardent hope is that he finds the green, green grass overlooked by both his father and his grandfather.

CAMP GREENBRIER

It's difficult to think of a small town as an enigma—large cities, with a diversity of culture, people and business, but not a small town and particularly a small town in the mountains of West Virginia. Nevertheless, I can tell you, without reservation, that Alderson, West Virginia was, and probably still is, an enigma.

During the early part of this century, Alderson was a booming railroad town, with a college, a military academy, a women's federal prison, a camp for boys, and a multiplicity of diverse businesses. But, the decline of the railroad, the lack of modern highways and the limited vision of the town fathers resulted in the loss, one by one, of the schools and businesses which marked the town's success. Finally, in the late forties and the early fifties, the time of my youth, the federal prison and Camp Greenbrier were the only active landmarks remaining.

As a boy of twelve or thirteen, I was in awe of both the federal prison and Camp Greenbrier, probably because both were off limits to townspeople. My father worked as a guard at the prison for a time and many of my friends' parents were employed at the prison. As a result, most of the young men had ambivalent feelings about the prison. Camp Greenbrier, however, was another matter.

Camp Greenbrier was specifically designed to attract young boys with wealthy parents, mostly from the large cities, who would spend the summer months, generally doing remedial school work and "roughing it". They lived in tents with electric lights and wood floors, sleeping on army cots and walking to the latrine—buildings equipped with indoor plumbing and showers.

The camp bordered the river, with a view of the woods and mountains in all directions. The campers were introduced to horseback riding, archery, target shooting, swimming and canoeing in a structured, semi-military environment. Most attended one or more classes during the week, either advanced or remedial.

A core of educators, from at least two different universities, operated the camp, assisted by college students, mostly gifted athletes who used the afternoon rest periods to practice their chosen sport, generally football. The educators lived in houses and the counselors in cabins within the camp complex.

The campers were not allowed outside of the camp complex, unless accompanied by a counselor; however, the off duty counselors were free to roam the town at their leisure, except during periods when their safety was threatened, which was most of the time.

Most of the counselors attended prestigious colleges and universities, were well traveled and came to this rural area of West Virginia with a certain air of superiority. And, most of the townspeople had never even visited a college or university or traveled more than one hundred miles from home. This contrast, if nothing more, provided the basis for conflict.

But the local girls, many of whom had local boyfriends, were the real problem. There was a natural attraction between the young college counselors and the local high school girls or those recently graduated, an attraction which caused friction, sometimes resulting in fights, between the counselors and the local males. Accordingly, every Summer brought with it a renewed animosity between the campers and the townspeople.

And, the local policeman, with overactive hormones and an abnormal attraction for young women, was of no help. Actually, he was a frequent instigator of the trouble between the campers and the town boys, though never a participant. He knew full well that the counselors would be confined to the campgrounds in the event of the slightest trouble. This left the policeman free to flirt with and proposition all of the young females with little competition from the counselors or the local boys who spent their time conjuring up ways of getting even with the counselors.

Over the years, it became a ritual for all of the males between the age of twelve and eighteen to harass the campers with some regularity. Each night the young men of the town met at the end of the bridge and related tales of their exploits or of the exploits of others, past and present. Each incident was recounted with great embellishment. As a result, local reputations were made, and sometimes lost, at the end of the bridge.

Hurling rocks or apples at the rows of tents, mostly late at night, was a favorite form of harassment. No one was ever hurt, but the sound of rocks or apples landing on the tents was certain to scare the young campers out of their wits and create confusion within the camp complex.

Sometimes, during the afternoon rest periods, when the campers were in their tents and the counselors were at the athletic field practicing football, two or three of the town boys would sneak up the riverbank or swim the width of the river and push several of the canoes from the riverbank into the water, often riding the canoes or swimming alongside the canoes, until they were finally abandoned to the river current. The town boys would quickly swim to the opposite side of the river and walk or run to the bridge several hundred yards downstream where they would await the parade of the counselors. Within a half hour, several of the counselors in the remaining canoes could be seen paddling downstream toward the bridge to retrieve the unguided canoes set loose by the local boys. Others would gather on the bridge, yelling at the counselors as they came near or passed under the bridge.

The camp had two docks—one anchored at the riverbank and another in the middle of the river. Ropes with buoys connected the two docks and the dock in the center of the river was anchored by ropes attached to large iron anchors laying at the river's bottom. The enclosed area between the docks formed the swimming hole for the campers.

The docks were a favorite attraction for the town boys. At least once each Summer, two or three of the town boys, armed with hunting knives, would swim the width of the river, generally after dark, to the outer dock, cutting all of the ropes and thereby freeing the outer dock to float downstream toward the bridge. Early the next morning, a mass of counselors in canoes could be seen surrounding the dock, frantically paddling upstream with the dock in tow. Everyone crossing the bridge would smile, knowing that two or three of the young town boys had just been elevated to hero status.

After a few Summers, the camp owners got smart and anchored the outer dock with heavy metal chains. This worked for a short time, until the town boys learned to swim with and use chain cutters. Thereafter, the ritual continued.

For young boys, there are two languages—English and cussing. I became bilingual at an early age, and at twelve or thirteen, cussing became my mother language. It was much easier than English since a single cuss word could be used as a noun, a verb or an adverb, all in one sentence. All of my friends were similarly bilingual.

One Saturday afternoon, with nothing much to do, three of my friends and I decided to sneak up the riverbank on the camp side, dive from the diving board attached to the main dock at the camp's swimming area and swim the width of the river, at the same time making lots of noise to attract the campers and counselors. It was the campers' rest period. We were, therefore, confident that the campers would be in their tents and the counselors would be on the athletic field.

We were in a line, bent forward, slowly following a narrow path along the riverbank, whispering cuss words with every step, when suddenly four very large counselors emerged from the thicket, two in front and two behind us, blocking any hope of escape. They led us to the main dock, sat us down, quietly lectured us on the stupidity of cussing and the evils attendant to harassing young boys who were raised in different environments and who were in utter fear of the mountains and the townspeople, urging us to empathize with the young campers who were quite out of their element. To say that we were scared would be an understatement. We were in fear for our lives, even with the quiet tone of the lectures and the outward friendliness of our captors.

Finally, the lectures complete, one of the captors told us we could swim in the camp swimming area and even use the diving board, if we didn't make an inordinate amount of noise. They then turned and walked toward the tents, leaving us in silence to ponder what had just transpired and to individually feel the guilt from our past misdeeds. We each dived once from the diving board, then retraced the path along the riverbank to town. None of us ever harassed the campers again.

A few weeks later I again saw my captors, all four of them, playing baseball with the town baseball team. Thanks to the athleticism of these counselors, the local baseball team handily won most, if not all, of its baseball games. Over the remainder of that Summer, the animosity between the townspeople and Camp Greenbrier dissolved—so much so that these two former enemies, for the most part, have lived in peaceful coexistence ever since.

The next Fall I learned the true identity of two of the captors. One was Bill Wade, then quarterback for the Vanderbilt football team, later to become quarterback for the Chicago Bears. His brother, Don Wade, who played center for the Vanderbilt team was another. I never knew anything about the other two, except that they were both superb athletes.

Don Wade died a short time later in a tragic accident. The life of Bill Wade was remarkable and I suspect, the lives of the unknown captors was equally remarkable in their own right, but their true legacy will likely be the manner in which their lives touched the lives of others, not in the public arena, but privately, without fanfare and without the expectation of reward.

Ironically, our lives are forever marked, not necessarily by great events, but by people, good and bad, sometimes in small, almost forgotten segments of time.

THE DOG BREEDERS

The most depressing years of a man's life are the two years after his thirteenth birthday, when he's too old to play Cowboys and Indians and too young for a meaningful job. The half boy/half man is destined to continually roam his world for a new adventure, biding time for the day when his manhood ripens and he is accepted by the boys in high school as an equal or, at least, a near equal. During those years, the boy/man feels a strange, new sexuality; yet, he's not sure what it is and he doesn't quite know what to do with it. As one of the boys at the end of the bridge said, "Finally, I've got lead in my pencil, but there ain't no girl I can write to."

Jimmy Rowe, my best friend, and I were no different. We spent most of our time, particularly during the summer months, roaming our world, searching for some new adventure. We made the rounds of the town, chatting with those store owners or employees who would talk to us, or stopping at the railroad station to watch people board or exit the passenger trains, sometimes looking at those who remained and wondering who they were, what they did or where they were going.

In our travels, Jimmy and I frequently passed the home of John Mirax, an old black man, bent double from arthritis or the burdens of his world or by his own preference, who spent all of his waking hours remodeling his old home, a ramshackle old structure, untouched by the hand of an architect or decorator but to it's owner, a magnificent building, constructed by his own hands.

John routinely raided houses under construction, just after the construction crew finished their days work, hauling to his home all of the scrap lumber, nails, electrical wire and other materials abandoned by the workmen. He carried his materials in a rather large wagon, customized to aid the old man in his chores. All of the contractors knew about John's raids but made no effort to stop him; and, it was common knowledge that the workmen left materials for John to find.

The old builder stockpiled the materials in his back yard for use on his current project, his next project or the one after that, since Mirax Construction Company was continually tearing out an existing room or adding another room to the dilapidated old house. A montage of sidings covered the outside walls, and the roof was layered with shingles of every kind and color.

We always spoke to John. In turn, John would raise his face, smile and nod, but would rarely speak. He didn't need to. The smile and the sparkle of his yellowish eyes said it all. The old man was living in a different world—a world we couldn't envision or comprehend.

Housby Brothers Construction Company, the largest construction company in the area, specializing in constructing quality homes. Jimmy and I were well acquainted with the owners of the company as well as all of the workmen. Having no particular agenda, we stopped at the construction sites several times each week, to view the construction and share stories with the workmen.

One day, while walking past one of the construction sites, Jimmy yelled, "Hey, Grayson. I understand that you graduated from the John Mirax School of Construction." (Grayson was one of the Housby brothers.)

I heard a voice from a shadowy figure reply, "Little bastard," as the workmen roared with laughter. Then, Grayson stepped out of the shadows with a grin on his face, which told us that he wasn't angry. We walked on, seeking a new adventure.

Between adventures, we scoured the town in search of a glimpse of Glenna Grose, known as "Lovie" by her friends and relatives. She was the most beautiful woman I had ever seen. She had Hollywood blond hair and golden tanned skin that covered a perfectly formed body. But her walk was the best part of her. As one of the boys at the end of the bridge remarked, "There ain't a fifty dollar mare in all of West Virginia what's got a better walk than Lovie Grose." All of the other boys, displaying a sort of nocturnal smile, nodded their assent.

With her sultry walk, Lovie always strode past us as if we didn't exist. I always expected her to speak, but, then, why should a beautiful seventeen year old girl acknowledge the existence of two scruffy thirteen year old boys.

After a glimpse of Lovie, Jimmy and I, giddy from the sight of the most captivating woman who ever lived, tried to regain our composure by planning our next adventure. What about a walk to "rock bar," a favorite swimming hole, about a mile upriver from the center of town, where most of the young women frequently gathered to sunbathe or swim, or maybe we could walk to "anvil rock," located another half mile upstream, where the older boys tested their manhood by jumping from the crest of the large rock— that had the appearance of a blacksmith's anvil—to the deep water below. How about a trip to the jail where we could swap stories with the prisoners or the railroad station or the shoe repair shop or maybe some place we had never been...? We always chose some adventure that was familiar to both of us—something we had done dozens of times before.

Then, one early morning in mid summer, Jimmy arrived at my house. Winded and exhausted from running and from his excitement, Jimmy, in something of a stutter, said, "I've been awake damned near all night thinking about how we could make some money. This morning, I looked at old G.I. Joe lying on the floor next to my bed and realized that the answer was right there before my eyes." G.I. Joe was Jimmy's big yellow dog who followed us on all of our adventures. Jimmy's dad often said, "Old Joe's pure bred—a pure bred mongrel, with the blood of every breed of dog that ever lived running through his veins." Anyway, I was totally confused. How could making money have anything to do with Joe?

Jimmy continued, "All we got to do is find us a bitch dog in heat.

We'll beat off the male dogs following her, take her to the shed out back of our house and breed her with Joe. After a time... I don't know how long... the bitch will have a bunch of puppies. All will look exactly like Joe. We can sell each of the Puppies for twenty five or thirty dollars. Hell, we'll be rich. Who wouldn't want a dog that'll grow up exactly like Joe."

"But, how do you find a bitch in heat?" I replied.

Jimmy responded like I was some kind of idiot, "You look for a dog followed by a bunch of other dogs. The first dog is the bitch and the rest are the male dogs trying to mate with the bitch."

"How can you be sure that the puppies will look like Joe and not like the bitch dog?" With this question I was able to discover the source of Jimmy's grand plan.

Jimmy said, "Joe Henry Johnson stopped by the house the other night and had a few drinks with dad. They got to talking about dog breeding, and, you know, Joe Henry knows everything about dogs and dog breeding. He said that, like humans, most of the pups will look like the father."

At this point, I was really skeptical. I pointed out that I had black hair and greenish brown eyes, like my mother, and that my father was blond with blue eyes. Then, it occurred to me, my brother and my two sisters were blond with blue eyes.

"That's what Joe Henry was talking about. I'm the spit'n image of my dad and he looks exactly like his dad. Joe Henry calls those who look like their mother mootashuns. I think the word came from a study they did on cows. Anyway, you're what they call a mootashun. It just means that you ain't normal."

I felt like I had just been hit with a ton of bricks. With my black hair and greenish brown eyes, I had always known that I was different from my father and my siblings, and while my brother and sisters had always treated me kindly, I recognized that they had a bond with each other that I would never experience. I now knew that I was a mootashun, a genetic abnormality.

In the coming weeks, I looked at everyone I met, thinking, "Is this a normal person or a mootashun?" I became consumed with the paranoia of my birth.

In the meantime, Jimmy and I were in constant search for the proper mate for G.I. Joe. Armed with baseball bats and a rope looped at one end, Jimmy and I, accompanied by the old yellow dog, scoured the town for weeks, in search of a bitch dog in heat. Then, by accident, we saw a black dog, slightly smaller than Joe, followed by several dogs of different breeds, colors and sizes. It was just like Jimmy described, and the dogs were within a block of Jimmy's home.

Startled by Joe's growl, the male dogs stopped and directed their attention to Joe. At first, all of the male dogs began growling and barking, then a couple attacked Joe, but they were no match for the big yellow dog. During the fight, Jimmy walked over to the bitch dog, looped the rope around her neck and started walking her toward his house. One after another, the male dogs realized that their prize was being taken away.

All of the male dogs started after Jimmy and the bitch—barking, growling and snapping at Jimmy's legs. Using the baseball bats and with the help of Joe, we were able to lead the black dog to a utility building behind Jimmy's house. Somehow, Jimmy got the bitch dog and Joe into the shed and closed the door. I continued beating off the other male dogs, who still had some hope of success until the door to the shed closed. After a few minutes, the male dogs left, one by one, and Jimmy and I were left to witness the commencement of our new business.

Several years later, I discovered that a good looking woman at a bar, surrounded by several male suitors, mirrored our experience with the bitch dog in heat followed by her suitors. The scent of a female frequently causes a male to momentarily lose his sanity. This is true with dogs and with men.

Proud of ourselves, we peered through the side window of the utility building, watching the two dogs sniff each other for a few minutes. Without fanfare, Joe mounted the back of the black dog and humped a few times, then stopped, and in something of a contortion, swung one of his rear legs over the back of the bitch. The dogs were standing rear to rear, obviously in a canine afterglow.

Suddenly, Jimmy exclaimed, "Damn, they're stuck and Mama's due home in ten minutes. If she finds us breeding dogs, she'll beat the hell out of me." Without explanation, he ran into the house, and after several minutes, returned with a large pot of boiling water. Carefully holding the large pot with pot holders, Jimmy waddled into the shed as I held the door. Jimmy dumped the entire pot of water onto the ass end of both dogs, who howled in pain and danced around the shed floor.

Then, Joe, the bigger dog, raced out of the shed, dragging the bitch dog behind him. The dogs were still stuck as they raced up the hill, made their way through a barbed wire fence, and continued to run until they were out of our sight.

Jimmy stared toward the top of the hill, stunned by the fact that he had hurt his constant companion and the realization that he may never see Joe again. There was nothing I could say or do, so I turned and walked away in an effort to mask the lump in my throat.

Several days later, Joe returned, followed by the black dog. Joe looked terrible. Patches of his yellow hair were missing and he walked with a noticeable limp. On the other hand, the black dog walked with a certain pride, seemingly telling all of the world that she was now Joe's mate.

With the consent of Jimmy's mother, the two dogs set up housekeeping in the shed behind Jimmy's house. Jimmy named the black dog "Isabel," evidently in an effort to keep all of his friends from referring to her as the black bitch. After all, she was now Joe's mate, soon to be the mother of his puppies.

Jimmy and I checked on Joe and Isabel every afternoon and shared our dreams about what we were going to do with the money from the sale of the puppies. By our standards, we were damned near rich, somewhat like the men who invest in the stock market or place their money in gambling devices in Las Vegas.

Finally, about six weeks after the honeymoon, I went to Jimmy's house to find him in deep despair. Fighting off tears, Jimmy said, "Our dog breedin' business has gone straight to hell." I followed him to the shed and saw what he was talking about. There on a blanket were Isabel and six black puppies, all mootashuns—all just like me.

The irony was more than I could comprehend. As I walked home, there was a new spring in my step, and my laughter could be heard for several blocks. "Damn Joe Henry Johnson and damn his voodoo genetics," I thought. For the first time in weeks, I again felt normal... normal, that is, for a mootashun.

COM-AH-NE-AH-SA

And they were filled with the Holy Ghost,
and began to speak with other tongues.
The Acts of the Apostles 2:3,4

I am convinced that I have total immunity from the forces of lightning. I could play golf in the most horrific thunderstorm and never be touched by a bolt of lightning. I could even clutch a lightning rod, stand beneath a tree in a storm or climb a metal tower knowing that lightning will never touch me, for if God had seen fit to strike me with lightning, he would have done so when I was sixteen or seventeen years of age.

During that time, a large tent was erected on a vacant lot, two doors from the pool room adjacent to the main highway running through my home town. At the end of the bridge, the gathering place for most of the town's young men, there was a buzz of speculation. By the end of the day, the tent was in place, folding chairs had been placed in rows separated by two aisles, a podium placed at the front and a large sign installed outside which read, "REVIVAL."

I was familiar with the term "revival," but I was always a little confused by the term. In the Old Greenbrier Baptist Church, where I was a member, we had a revival every year or so. A guest minister would hold services every night during the week and all of the adults seemed to feel good because there had been a revival. But, I saw no difference in the people and concluded, in my own mind, that somehow you had to experience a "vival" before you could have a "revival", and except for a few of the members, I saw no evidence of a vival.

At that time in my life, I was unfamiliar with a tent revival, although

I have since discovered that the tent revival was commonplace, particularly in the rural areas. Moreover I was not quite prepared for a Pentecostal tent revival, which seemed to be a strange mixture of Christianity, voodoo and ancient tribal rites.

For the boys at the end of the bridge, the tent revival became the favorite pastime. Our curiosity was overwhelming. We never entered the tent or became a part of the festival, always electing to stand outside the tent as casual observers, but our view was clear since the sides of the tent were uncovered prior to the opening prayer, which always lasted about ten minutes, finally punctuated by the preacher gasping and sucking wind with each phrase or each word.

People came from miles away to become a part of the revival. Most were strangers, which was not unusual since most of my friends and acquaintances, young and old, were either Baptist, Methodist, Presbyterian or heathen, the latter forming the larger group.

A couple of hours before each meeting, a workman would lay a three inch carpet of new straw in front of the podium and down each aisle. This confused me, at first. Later, it became perfectly clear. The straw cushion or carpet was installed to prevent injury to some of the more jubilant members of the audience, who became filled with the Holy Ghost and in a frenzy began rolling and thrashing about in the straw, ostensibly without self control.

Pentecostal music was then, and has always been, intriguing to me. Most Pentecostals are not musically trained; yet, their music is generally superior to the music of most other congregations. It's happy music, evidently learned from early age. If you find four Pentecostal babies in a nursery, they will cry in harmony. And, a Pentecostal without a tambourine is not worth his or her salt. This was made clear at the first meeting where the music was provided by two guitars, a mandolin, a set of drums and at least a dozen tambourines, forming a background for the singer or singers. Surprisingly, the unusual sound produced by this mix of instrumentation was quite good, although a little heavy on the tambourines. But, the audience seemed pleased, as did the singers.

The individual singers usually sang slow songs with a lot of meaning and passion, calculated to bring tears to a glass eye. On the other hand, the quartets, for the most part sang upbeat, happy songs which made you want to jump up and shout or dance, and the trios sang something in between. The minister, in total charge of the Revival, orchestrated his performance with the individual singers, quartets and trios to perfection to bring about the mood or emotion of the moment.

One particular male quartet was my favorite and a favorite of the audience. Because of their talents and unique sound, everyone ignored their propensity for strong drink. In actuality, the quality of their sound and their total performance was directly related to the amount of alcohol consumed, and in their case, the more they drank, the better they performed. At least this was generally true. One night the minister announced that the quartet would not be performing because of the illness of the bass singer. He failed to announce that the bass singer began drinking too early in the day and was found in a drunken stupor about an hour before the meeting.

Every night, the fire breathing preacher, together with the music, was like hypnotism, working the crowd into a trance like state, which, in turn, brought in the Holy Spirit, producing unintelligible speech from the congregation as well as the minister. Someone would yell, "com-ah-ne-ah-sa", or so it sounded, followed by more peculiar words and sounds. This was called speaking in tongues or speaking in the unknown tongue, a gift provided by the Holy Spirit. The, people, male and female, would begin rolling and thrashing in the straw, first in the aisles, ultimately working their way to the area in front of the podium. Every so often, you could see people open one eye and glance around to see what their neighbors were doing or saying– then, returning to their own rituals after a brief glance.

Some fifteen minutes of rolling, thrashing, shouting and speaking in words never known to man, the audience returned to normalcy. This happened shortly after the Holy Spirit left the preacher.

Then came the matter of raising money for the work of the Lord, which might take anywhere from fifteen minutes to a one hour depending on the Holy Spirit's communication with the audience and the amount of money collected, which were really the same. This was followed by the parting song. The audience left in a weakened condition from the events of the past couple of hours but totally renewed—at least for a few hours.

The Pentecostal religion is as foreign to me now as it was then. Throughout my life, I have known many Christians whose faith and dedication are beyond any doubt whatsoever. Why, then, are these Christians—Baptist, Methodist, Presbyterian, Catholic, Church of Christ and others—not filled with the Holy Spirit to the extent that they lose all self control and begin speaking in tongues? This I have never understood. Nonetheless, the Pentecostal tent meetings often left me uplifted, with a greater sense of my own spirituality.

Moreover, these revivals proved to be an excellent source for meeting attractive girls. It was a revelation to discover that many of these young women had become sexually aroused during the services, a fact which completely escaped most of my friends—a fact I was not about to disclose.

Anyway, I was sorely disappointed to see the tent come down, marking the end of the revival. I don't suppose I could ever become a Pentecostal. The concept of speaking in tongues is completely foreign to my thought process. Yet, one day I might—*just might*—go out looking for an old time tent meeting where the music is good, the people speak in tongues and the women are a tad frisky after the service. After all, I am now totally immune from lightning.

THE RUBY RED CROSS

At the age of eleven, I left my father's funeral, dazed and confused, with no one to turn to and no place to hide; and at that particular time in my life, I desperately needed a hiding place—a place far from the meaningless chatter of the adults, a place where I could maybe commune with my father. More than anything else, I needed to be near my father. Or, at least I needed to be near to my father's things.

So, at home after the funeral, while family and friends gathered to comfort each other, I quickly changed clothes, grasped the cigar box containing my father's personal effects, which were now my inheritance and, without notice, quickly left the house to find a place of solitude where I could commune with my father. The house, the place where my father had died a few days before, filled with people who were trying to say something profound but who lacked the right words. As I listened to all of the meaningless drivel, I had the sensation of being smothered. Outside, the cool, crisp air normalized my irregular breathing and cleared the cobwebs from my head.

I ran across the road in front of my house, through a neighbor's yard and up a steep, winding path to a large rock half way up the mountain which shadowed my house. Sitting on the rock, I opened the cigar box and began to inventory my inheritance, gently rubbing each item—as the fond memories of my father flooded my head—the white gold pocket watch, wound once daily by my father, the antique cuff links and tie clasp, with my father's initials (also mine), a knife, a hand carved ring custom made for my father by one of the inmates at the Women's Federal Prison and a ruby red cross mounted on a stick pin.

The pocket watch was given to me by my father just before
he died. The next day, my mother, in tears, handed me the rest of
my inheritance, without explanation. Of course, the watch was my
favorite. It had been passed directly from my father's hand to mine,
just before he took his last breath. I considered the transfer of the
watch from my father to me as a kind of sacred ceremony, a passing
of the torch, if you will, which served as an eternal bond between us.
At that time, the rest of my inheritance was of no consequence.

For a time, I did wonder about the ruby red cross. But, then, I
also wondered about the cuff links and tie clasp. I saw my father in
a coat and tie only on one or two occasions, mainly funerals of close
friends, and he did not own any shirts with french cuffs. Why, then,
would he need, or even want, cuff links, and why did he have the
ruby red cross?

The mystery of the cuff links and tie clasp was solved a few
weeks later. Sitting at the living room desk, looking at the cuff links,
I had not noticed my mother's presence until she spoke. "Those cuff
links and tie clasp are special," she said, "They were my gift to your
father on our wedding day." I asked about the ruby red cross but got
no response. This was not unusual. It was simply my mother's way.
I didn't press the issue. I reasoned that my mother would tell me
about the cross at some later time. She never did.

I frequently got out the old cigar box, surveyed my inheritance
and communed with my father—at least for a few years. Then, for
some reason, those times of communion with my father became less
frequent. Ultimately, the cigar box was replaced with a jewelry box
and the white gold pocket watch was placed on a watch stand. The
knife was lost during my youth; the cuff links and tie clip were much
too delicate for normal use; the ring was huge, even for my father's
large fingers; and, the ruby red cross never seemed appropriate,
either as a tie pin or a lapel pin. Consequently, those treasures of my
youth, having been entombed in my jewelry box, were for the most
part, relegated to the depths of my memory, except for the pocket
watch. The watch affixed to the watch stand was carefully located in

a prominent place on my desk at home as a constant reminder of my father.

My brother, Sheldon, and I were never close. It wasn't that we disliked each other or that we didn't have a desire to become close; it was more a matter of circumstance. My brother was fifteen years my senior, attending college, in military service and returning to college, during my formative years. He was one of the mass of veterans returning to the universities and colleges after World War II in search of the American Dream. After college, Sheldon moved to Florida, then to Arizona. As a result, we just didn't see each other.

Finally, my brother came to my home for a two week visit, almost thirty five years after my father's death. We were both anxious and exhilarated at the same time. During those two weeks, we formed a bond of sorts as we discussed our family and friends and the times of our youth. It was a beneficial visit for both of us.

During one of those conversations, as we spoke of our father, my brother said, "You know, I've wondered many times what happened to the ruby red cross stick pin. That's the one thing I wanted after Dad's death." I immediately went to my jewelry box, retrieved the stick pin and gave it to my brother, telling him that he now had his inheritance after all these years. Tears filled his eyes as he rubbed the cross, obviously reflecting with fond memories on those days with our father.

After a few minutes, I asked my brother about the significance of the ruby red cross. His answer was not what I expected, although I should have guessed the meaning of the cross many years before. Our father was a member of the Ku Klux Klan and the stick pin represented the firey red cross of the Klan.

I was absolutely mortified. That this kindly man, who treated both white and black as equal, who had many close black friends, and who never said the "N" word (at least to my knowledge)—that this gentle man was a member of the Klan, with all of its bigotry and hatred... well, this just couldn't be true. Yet, the ruby red cross itself suggested otherwise.

Sheldon went on to explain that the Klan, at least the Klan in our hometown, during the 1920s, was not the Klan as we understand it—prone to church burning, beating, mutilating and killing blacks—with a membership generally composed of near idiots. The Klan members in our town were some of the most respected members of the community. My brother recognized each of the Klan members from the shoes they wore and was quite certain of the identity of each member.

According to Sheldon, the Klan, at that time, in that particular town, was totally dedicated to justice in its most basic form, to the protection of the weak and to the preservation of the peace and tranquility of the community. I could relate to this explanation, sort of, but what about the threats and the violence? What about the cross burnings?

"Yes," my brother said, "There were cross burnings, and there was some violence, but probably more threats than violence; and there were, indeed, many people, both black and white, who were fearful of the Klan—most with good cause. When a cross was burned in your yard, this was notice that you had best change your behavior. And, the cross was burned only when a person had done something particularly bad—severely beating his wife or kids, not working without a reason and allowing his family to live in poverty, or habitual drunkenness—things that were detrimental to the good of the community."

My brother insisted that the Klan did not discriminate. The cross was burned on the land of the white man and the land of the black man, according to the person's bad deeds and without regard to race. And, those who were the real victims, the women, the children, the elderly, the oppressed, were appreciative and held the Klan in high regard.

Apparently, the Klan drastically changed during the 1930s, becoming more violent and more directed against blacks. It was then that my father, as well as most of the other good townsmen, quit the Klan. Within a short time, the Klan disbanded and was virtually nonexistent in the 1940s.

There was, however, one incident during the early 1950s which indicated that the Klan was alive, well and active. I remember the incident well. During the late Spring, a large cross was burned on top of one of the mountains, in full view of the entire town. The lone taxi was in great demand, transporting blacks and poor whites from the movie or work or the town businesses to their respective homes, generally, a distance of less than a mile. After a couple of months someone discovered that it was the owner of the taxi who burned the cross. It seems that his business had dropped off when the weather got warm and being an enterprising sort of fellow, the taxi owner saw the burning cross as a means of increasing his business. He was given a stern warning by the town policeman and the burning cross never reappeared.

I was not totally convinced of the honor and integrity of the Klan from my brother's accounts. Yet, I knew my father. At least, I knew the man who was my father during the first eleven years of my life, and that man was no Klansman. But, then, I'm not sure that I know what a Klansman is or is not. Moreover, I'm not sure that I know what my father was or was not. Now older, I suspect that my father was much like me and like most others I know. He was both good and bad.

For me, I will always remember the good in my father's life. I loved the man. He was my father, and while the firey red cross may have a different meaning for many different people, in my mind the ruby red cross attached to the stick pin will always represent the love and the kindness and the honor that was my father.

BIG MAN

Unlike most of my college classmates, my options for spring break were limited. Between money received from the G.I. Bill and from bartending five nights a week, I was able to pay room, board, tuition, books and out of state tuition, with just enough left over for automobile expenses and an occasional date. Therefore, any thoughts of joining the mass of caravans leaving the campus for Florida or South Carolina or some other exotic place, in something of a carnival atmosphere, were quickly dismissed. I was content to travel back to my home town where I knew I would be well fed and, best of all, entertained.

Entertainment in a small town is quite different from entertainment in a city. In a city, you go and do. In a small town, you find the common gathering place and there, with others you have known most of your life, tell stories and listen to the stories of others, laughing and joking and cussing and making fun, until the early hours of the next day. While most of the stories had been told and retold dozens of times, the last telling would always contain some new element, generally accepted without question by the audience. And, every so often, there would be a new story or maybe a new story in the making.

There were three gathering places in my home town—the pool room, and less than a block away, a billboard sign at the end of a concrete bridge, and "Mack's Snack Shack". The men within a decade of my age, mostly single, but not always, wandered between the pool room, "the end of the bridge" and "Mack's Snack Shack" in search of new stories and new information.

During my sophomore year of college, I arrived home shortly

before dusk, dumped my bags in the spare bedroom, which used to be my bedroom, and sat down at the kitchen table to watch my mother prepare the remainder of the feast to welcome her prodigal son back to the home place. I had already seen the loaves of salt rising bread and the four pies, as well as a roast, and several pots of vegetables. Without much conversation, my mother filled my plate, placed it in front of me and sat down at the opposite end of the table to watch me eat, asking every few seconds whether I wanted more roast, beans, bread, butter or anything else within my reach. I was always aggravated by this ritual, but I had learned that this was my mother's way of saying, "Welcome Home". After the second piece of pie, eaten solely because my mother thought I was losing too much weight, I excused myself, telling Mom that I would be back later. Without saying anything, she knew that it would be much later.

I walked from the house across the old bridge to the billboard sign at the "end of the bridge", and after greetings and some small talk, I took my rightful place in the group, while the stories, interrupted by my arrival, continued. Someone told the story of the village idiot who declared that the small apple pie purchased from the local grocery tasted good but that the crust was a little hard to eat. Then, someone recognized that he was eating the cardboard plate together with the pie. Although most of us were quite familiar with this story, we all laughed loud and long, as if the story had been told for the very first time. As the stories continued, I slipped away to Mack's Snack Shack for coffee, knowing that I would not be missed.

I joined a couple of high school girls, in a back booth and listened while each of the girls talked about leaving the boredom of this small town and going away to college. They spoke of college as if it were singular, located in a far off place and filled with beautiful, well dressed people, with bubbling personalities, leading exciting lives. I answered a series of pointed questions about this Camelot life I was supposed to be leading, but I wasn't exactly truthful. I told them what they wanted to hear. I didn't dare tell them about my classmate who wore G.I. brogans during the heat of the summer and flip flops with no socks in the snow, nor did I tell them about classes with more than a hundred students or the strange ideologies propounded by some of the professors. Their virgin minds were not ready. I smiled and excused myself, retreating to the "end of the bridge" and to other fantasies of the evening.

After listing to a couple of good jokes, three or four stories filled with half truths and one or two downright lies, I decided to visit the pool room. One of my old friends, Dick Smithson, met me outside the pool room, warning me to be careful. According to Dick, Big Man was in a fretful mood, a mood which usually led to a fight and no one wanted to fight with Big Man. "He's already drunk five or six beers and the crazy bastard always wants to fight when he's drunk. If you're going in there, don't upset him. I'm not hanging around. The last time I was drinking with Big Man I got hurt and I've got six stitches in my head to prove it." As Dick walked off into the night, I entered the pool room, against my better judgment.

Everyone knows everyone else in a small town, and although I hadn't seen Big Man in more than five years, I recognized him immediately. He stood about 6'4" and weighed maybe 250 pounds, with dirty blond hair and a ruddy complexion. He was wearing work pants, a plaid flannel shirt and old work boots. Grease marks streaked his face and his clothing. His hands were rough and discolored with the kind of dirt that soap and water cannot penetrate, and it was rather obvious that he hadn't shaved or bathed for several days.

To my surprise, Big Man lumbered toward me in a half stagger. Remembering Dick's advise, I almost turned and ran from the Pool Room. Instead of reaching out his hand, Big Man hugged me like I was a long, lost brother. I wondered if he even recognized me, as one of his giant hands wrapped around my wrist and pulled me to a bar stool. Big Man then ordered a couple of beers, insisted on paying and proceeded to reminisce about our good times in school.

I couldn't remember Big Man in school, but I didn't want to come right out and admit my memory lapse. He was, after all, in a jovial mood and I didn't want to risk changing that mood; yet, his recollections of school days were so general that I had no memory of those forgotten times. On the other hand, the twinkle in his eyes and the broad smile left no doubt that Big Man's memories were real, at least to him.

Several beers later, my apprehension completely subsided. "Now, Big Man," I said, "When was it that we had all of those good times in school?"

"Well," he replied, "It must have been somewhere around the third grade, cause that's the furthest I ever went."

Big Man and I talked about may things that night, during which time I formed a strange bond with my old friend. Did I experience those good times in school or did I even attend school with Big Man? I honestly didn't know.

On my drive back to the university, I thought about my life both during high school and at the university, and I thought about Big Man and his life. We were two completely different people forever bonded by the memories of only one of us. How I wished I had Big Man's memories.

THE RECRUITER

Denver Wellington Duff was the fourth child in a family of five or six or maybe seven children whose first names all started with the letter "D". He was born and raised, for the most part, on Muddy Creek Mountain, just outside Alderson, West Virginia—working, when he was not attending school, on his grandfather's farm.

His father, who had been a railroader, died at a relatively young age, a few years before Denver reached puberty, leaving his mother, Della, with a house full of stair-step children and no means of support, except for the charity of her father, Old Man Ed, a small government check and the good will of her siblings and friends. Old Man Ed's reasons for supporting Della and her band of children were more selfish than benevolent, for in the children Ed saw a band of workers to plant and harvest his crops. Ed reasoned, "If they can eat, they can work."

When Denver reached his teen age years, Old Man Ed sold the farm, except for a small tract of woodland, where the old man built a cabin of rough sawed wood with a metal roof consisting of one room and a path to an outhouse. There, the old man spent the rest of his life as a semi-hermit, rejecting almost everyone, except for his son, Roy, and Roy's family, which suited Denver just fine.

Della and her family moved to a rental house in town and Denver began his real life without the domination of the old man. Yet, the old man's influence had left an indelible mark on Denver, which would follow him for the rest of his life. The new freedom, after the earlier years of torment, made Denver want to play all of the time. Fun and jokes were a happy substitute for the years of labor. And, play he did.

Then, sometime during his junior year in high school, Denver realized that he had studied too little and played too much, as a result of which school was becoming more and more like life with Old Man Ed. Denver never actually quit school. He just quit going to school.

At first, his days were spent at the pool room, learning eight ball and nine ball with some success, interrupted from time to time by a few days manual labor, doing construction work to earn a little spending money or gambling money. Finding no purpose or meaning in his life, Denver decided that he must find a full time job, a steady job, but a job with honor and dignity where he could wear a white shirt and tie—a job that would allow his personality to flourish, without the back breaking strain of manual labor.

Denver was hired as an ambulance driver for Lobban Funeral Home, mostly transporting the sick and elderly to the doctor or to the hospital, and on occasion, bringing the dead to the funeral home to prepare for burial or assisting in the funeral and burial. His work with the sick and elderly was superb; however, Denver could not be around dead bodies. It was a mental thing. Often, when transporting a dead body back to the funeral home, Denver would travel at high rates of speed on the mountain roads, somehow irrationally concluding that he could outrun the dead body in the compartment behind him.

After a few months, he took off the shirt and tie and returned to the pool room, where he was greeted by his old friends who had missed the practical jokes and the humorous stories.

At the time, the United States was engaged in a "police action" with North Korea. It seemed like a war, and for most of America, it was a war. Young men were leaving for military service and dead bodies or maimed servicemen were shipped home from Korea on a regular basis. Yet, the politicians insisted that it was merely a "police action", and so it was.

One night, after consuming almost a six pack of beer capped off by a couple of shots of whiskey, Denver stood on the bar at the pool room and commanded everyone's attention. In an emotional voice, he said, "Look at us. Drinking beer. Playing pool. Most of us without jobs. None of us have any purpose in our life. Doesn't anyone realize that our country needs us. Damn it, we're at war. I don't know about the rest of you, but I'm going to Beckley and join the Army tonight." Several of the good old boys agreed, and a total of five left for Beckley, West Virginia to join the Army.

Arriving at the Recruiting Station in Beckley, West Virginia, shortly after midnight, the five were assigned bunks for the remainder of the night. 5:00 a.m. came early and the breakfast which followed was not very palatable for those suffering from a hangover. After breakfast, the five warriors and a dozen other recruits were taken to the meeting room of the Recruiting Station for a "swearing in" ceremony. On the way, Denver slipped out of a side door and was back home before 9:00 a.m. The others were on their way to boot camp.

Denver repeated his practical joke two more times before the original group came home on leave following basic training. The reunion of the original warriors went rather well until all had consumed several bottles of beer. Then, the suppressed anger came out. One declared that Denver would either die or go to the Army. One thing led to another until the four took charge of Denver, drove him to Beckley and remained with him until after the swearing in ceremony. At last, Denver became a private in the United States Army and the Recruiting Station in Beckley, West Virginia, lost its best recruiter.

THE APPLEFEST
CIRCA 1952

No self respecting male ever left my hometown for more than a weekend without stopping by the local poolroom to say goodbye to his friends. It was a ritual of long standing, probably preceding the great war. And during the early 1950s it seemed as though someone was leaving town almost every day.

Growing up in rural West Virginia was an unbelievable experience, but little work was available. As a result, there was a mass exodus of those who left school by graduation or otherwise. The high school graduates, who for one reason or another did not leave for college, generally migrated to Washington, D.C., Richmond or Roanoke, Virginia, or some other city less than a days drive from home.

On the other hand the non-graduates often went to Detroit (pronounced Dee-troit) or Columbus, Ohio (pronounced Lumbus), lured northward by high paying factory jobs. For those seeking the factory jobs, the move was never meant to be permanent. They expected to work just long enough to be laid off and qualify for union benefits, company benefits or unemployment benefits, generally referred to as "rocking chair".

It was a Fall night shortly after Halloween when Wire, after consuming a half-pint of cheap whiskey and several bottles of beer, ambled over to one of the three pool tables and made his announcement. While it was not unusual for those in their teens, twenties or even thirties to leave town in search of a great adventure, everyone was completely shocked when Wire, who had never been more than fifty miles from home, except for his time in the army, in his forty or so years, suddenly announced that he was tired of working for nothing wages and that he was leaving for Dee-troit in about an hour, if he could borrow enough money for gas. After a moment of silence, someone passed the hat for the gas money. Everyone contributed as though his contribution would fund a great crusade.

After sufficient gas money had been raised, Mocas declared that he was joining the crusade, which was no surprise, since Mocas was probably the only automobile savant in town. He could rebuild an engine with baling wire and chewing gum. Somehow an old engine would purr as if repaired and tuned by a master mechanic. Everyone called it the "Mocas Touch."

Mocas thought of everything in terms of cars and racing. He had always been that way. As a child he made engine noises before he learned to talk. In a restaurant he would order dual hamburgers and twin milk shakes. It was probably a Godsend, then, that Mocas decided to make the long journey with Wire, for Wire's 1938 Chevrolet, which always needed repair and probably a visit from Orkin, would most certainly need some attention along the way.

Seemingly a minor event, the departure of Wire and Mocas, turned into a miniature festival. The travelers were fed like Kings at "Mack's Snack Shack", a local eatery near the pool room and later treated to three or four more bottles of beer at the pool room. At the height of the send-off, someone contributed two bushels of apples, carefully placed in the trunk of the car, next to the paper bags containing a change of clothes for each of them.

At last Wire and Mocas bid goodbye to those of us who would remain behind, somewhat jealous and longing for a similar adventure. Wire staggered to the old car, took the wheel and turned the ignition. There was a loud backfire and blue smoke bellowed from the exhaust, after which the old car surged forward, weaving northward. After the light from the one good tail light passed out of sight, there was almost complete silence, much like the silence after the fireworks on the Fourth of July.

For months thereafter those left behind regularly gathered at the poolroom to discuss the events of the day, tell jokes, venture a guess about the welfare of Wire and Mocas and ultimately recount the events surrounding their departure. There was never any news concerning the crusaders, probably because writing was as foreign to Wire and Mocas as was their new surroundings in Motown.

Finally, after eight or nine months, Wire and Mocas returned home to draw their "rocking chair". But, the homecoming was completely different than anyone expected. We expected Wire and Mocas to spend hours telling of their adventures in Dee-troit. Instead, there was a strained silence. Their faces were drawn and sallow, and their eyes were haunting, like some of the soldiers who came back from World War II. Everyone felt cheated, after all we were the ones who financed the great expedition.

To this day all of the Dee-troit puzzle has never been put together. In the following weeks, however, Wire or Mocas made little revelations which left little doubt about their journey or their stay in the Motor City.

Having spent their entire lives in the womb-like environment of rural West Virginia, the boys were not ready for the big city. Wire got a job within a couple of days. Although he was better qualified for employment in the automotive industry, Mocas was not so lucky. It was almost two weeks before Mocas found employment. According to Wire, Mocas would walk into an employment office with a chew of tobacco in his mouth, his hands in the hip pockets of his bib overalls and shout, "Hirin' anybody?" As a result, Mocas rarely got to the application stage.

But, this was only a part of the problem. You see, both Wire and Mocas believed that they would drive to Dee-troit, get a job the next day and rent a room on credit. They also believed that they would be paid at the end of each day. Of course, it didn't happen that way. After securing a job, the first paycheck came two weeks later and landlords refused to rent rooms, even on a week to week basis, without two weeks rent deposit. As a result, the boys slept in the car, washed at gas station rest rooms and ate apples until Wire's first paycheck arrived which allowed money for food. A rented room was not possible until Mocas had been employed for more than two weeks. By this time, the boys had slept in the old car, which was without gasoline, for more than a month, surviving the first snow of the season and walking miles for interviews or for work.

Piecing together the Motown experience, we were all relieved that we had not traveled with Wire and Mocas on their expedition to the north. At first, we treated the crusade with humor, ordering apple pie for Wire at "Mack's Snack Shack." It didn't seem quite so humorous, when Wire took one look at the apple pie, became violently ill and ran outside to vomit, or when both Wire and Mocas refused to leave the warmth of their homes during a snow.

After the great expedition, Wire and Mocas were never quite the same. They never laughed much and their facial expressions were always stoic. There was a hollowness in their eyes, and if you looked deep into their eyes, it almost seemed as if you were looking at the back of their head. They were like the prisoners of war who came out of the German or Japanese prison camps after World War II. They were the prisoners of Dee-troit.

One thing was certain. These two Prisoners never, ever ate an apple, or any food containing an apple, after the great expedition.

THE JAPANESE ATTACK ON ALDERSON, WEST VIRGINIA

In the early '40s, before television, there was nothing worse than a Sunday afternoon during the winter months, and for a six year old boy with an unbridled energy and an inquisitive nature, those afternoons were almost unbearable.

I was lounging on the couch in the small living room above the family restaurant, watching my father scan the radio for news or weather, trying, without success, to control my boredom. After a time, my incessant questions about anything and everything had driven my father into one of his "Sunday afternoon moods"—a time when every one of my questions would be answered with a grunt. He simply tuned me out. Psychologists refer to this behavior as an escape mechanism which allows parents to survive those years of parenting children from the age of two to about ten. After the age of ten, most children have no interest in questioning his parent about anything.

My father found a news station and I drifted off into my daydreams. After a few minutes, the voice on the news report changed to an animated, high pitched voice, speaking in unintelligible phrases, such as "yellow as an orange", followed by a series of numbers.

"That doesn't make any sense," I said, "an orange isn't yellow."

My daddy growled, "Hush, son. It must be some sort of code." The gibberish continued for what seemed like hours. Then, a calm, deep voice announced, "The Japanese have attacked Pearl Harbor."

December 7, 1941, was a pivotal day for everyone in my world. Within a few days, my older brother came home from college and immediately left for the army. My father tried to join the army, but was rejected because of his health. Almost everyone, it seemed, between the age of eighteen and forty left for military service within a couple of months, as a result of which the small, rural West Virginia town was transformed into a town of women, children and old men.

It wasn't long before certain food items and gasoline were rationed and ration coupons became as valuable as money. Since my family was in the restaurant business, my father often traded for sugar and butter coupons or bartered with the local farmers for "real" butter, after my mother declared that she couldn't bake a pie with that "fake" butter they called margarine.

Alderson, West Virginia, in the '40s was a bustling railroad town, even with the absence of it's young men. The coal driven trains now carried troops, military weapons, machinery and the dead bodies of America's young men, along with civilian passengers and various goods and merchandise for the general population. As a result, watching the passing trains and going to the railroad station for the scheduled train stops, became a ritual, especially for the young boys.

The concrete bridge, which connected the two sides of town, was also a favorite meeting place for both young and old, particularly on Sunday afternoons. There, the news would be disseminated among the townspeople—news of the dead and wounded and news of the location of our boys in service scattered throughout the world, most of which was information from the barbershop, the pool room or one of the women's hair emporiums scattered throughout the little village. Suddenly the world had become much smaller, with places in England, Germany, France and small islands in the pacific referred to as commonly as nearby towns, although most of the people had no concept of where those places were, since few had traveled more than fifty miles from home during their entire lives.

Even the village idiot talked about the Germanmen and Hungrymen with authority; and, as he held a newspaper upside down, featuring a picture of a sunken ship, *The USS West Virginia*, he declared, "No wonder it sunk. I can't figure out how the damned thing ever floated in the first place."

One Sunday afternoon, sometime after the first year of the war, my father and I were walking toward the bridge, where dozens of people had gathered for the weekly news, when I heard a woman yell, "The Japs are attacking! The Japs are attacking!" Then, I saw a small plane fly over the bridge and circle overhead. People immediately began yelling and screaming, some running while others fell face down on the sidewalk. It was complete chaos.

The small plane made a second pass over the bridge and again circled. This time, it looked like it flew under the bridge, although the pilot later stated that he never flew under the bridge. With each pass, the screaming got worse. Those on the bridge were convinced that the Japanese were, indeed, commencing their attack on Alderson, West Virginia. Finally, the plane flew off to the east, without ever firing a shot or dropping a bomb. Alderson was again safe from the dreaded enemy.

A few days later, reports were received that one of the local boys, who had become a Marine pilot, while on a flight from his home base in Elk City, Oklahoma to a base somewhere in the northeast decided to veer from his flight plan and buzz the bridge. His plane developed engine trouble and he had to land in Roanoke, Virginia.

The pilot, Leonard Hampton, never realized that he had created such fear among the townspeople. He simply intended to greet the people he knew and loved. Although some reports of the incident were made to the local politicians, the politicians apparently didn't know who to contact, or if they did, realized that the reporting process would be too cumbersome, particularly in view of the fact that no harm was done. Leonard was safe. His superiors never knew about the Japanese attack on Alderson, West Virginia.

This incident, as frightening as it was for those on the bridge and as humorous as it was for those who told the story over and over at the end of the bridge, brought about a new sense of patriotism among the townspeople and a new resolve to make any sacrifice necessary to win the war. The people of this small, mountain town had now been confronted with the perceived realism of war. They now knew that no sacrifice was too great for freedom. And, it was all due to a young man who decided to fly over his home town and greet his friends. *Semper Fi.*

THE WEST COAST PANTS

I grew up in an age when men wore coats and ties, at least to church and special events, when women wore dresses almost everywhere, when musical groups and musicians were not named after bugs or states or animals or food, i.e., The Beatles, Alabama, Snoop Doggy Dog, Meatloaf, etc., when a man's waist was thought to be several inches above his crotch and when the words of a song were easily identifiable. Well, almost. I was confused for a time with "I Rene Goodnight". Frankly, I didn't know how to rene goodnight, and I was quite certain that I had never rened goodnight, either alone or with any other person. Then there was the song "Return to Cinda", which totally confused me. How can you return to Cinda when her address is unknown? But for the most part, life was pretty well defined, and more importantly, understandable.

It was a time when people said "swell", as in "I had a swell time," or, "That was a swell movie." With some exceptions, children had a certain respect for their parents, even the unfit parents, and the standards of society were taught and maintained by the family, and strengthened by the schools, the churches and the movies. Movie stars set fashion trends, leaving politics to those more qualified, and news reporters were content with reporting the news rather than making the news. The courts interpreted the law, rather than creating the law. Workers were bound to work a full day for their pay and employers considered it a duty to preserve employment for those workers.

Then came the Zoot Suit, a West Coast/New York aberration of the male dress suit, which marked the transitional period in the great revolution which totally transformed western culture. Penny loafers were exchanged for blue suede shoes, then for tennis shoes or athletic shoes. Straight leg pants were traded for pegged pants, then tight blue jeans, always worn with a certain facial grimace and finally baggy shorts that covered the knees, with the waist firmly set approximately two inches below the crotch. Women replaced their dresses with tight jeans, probably designed by the makers of "Monostat 7" and baggy sweatshirts. Later, a large segment of the population, both men and women, seemingly replaced their entire wardrobe with sweatsuits, usually with designer or manufacturer or school or athletic team inscriptions to insure the individuality of the person. In keeping with the changing attire, melodic songs were discarded for Rock and Roll and now Rap, a complete bastardization of both word and music. And, it all happened because of the Zoot Suit.

The mark of the Zoot Suit was the jacket, with broad shoulders, narrowing to an almost nothing waist and extending in length to three or four inches above the knee. The pants were baggy at the hips and thighs, but tapered below the knees to a cuff barely large enough for a naked foot to pass through.

Generally, the Zoot Suit was worn with blue suede shoes, a long watch chain, looped from the belt to the knee and back to the front pocket where a cheap watch called a "dollar dummy" was attached. A hand-painted necktie and a pork pie hat, with a wide brim and a flat top, completed the attire. There was no mistaking a man in a Zoot Suit.

At the age of sixteen I longed for a Zoot Suit with the blue suede shoes, the watch chain and the pork pie hat, but I had little money and the one clothing store in my home town didn't sell those "devil clothes." Nevertheless, I was determined. With my initial savings I bought a pair of blue suede shoes and a wire suede shoe brush. Next, I focused on the pants. After a long month of anticipation I hitch hiked to a nearby town which boasted the best men's store in the area. Money in hand I entered the store ready to be transformed into the modern man.

A well dressed man approached and introduced himself as Izzy. I later learned that Izzy owned the store. I described the pants as best I could, and Izzy brought out several pair of pants, announcing, with authority, that these pants were the latest from the West Coast. I was shocked to discover that all of the pant legs were wide at the bottom. My disappointment must have shown, because I remember hearing Izzy saying, "Don't worry about the pant legs. We have the tailor taper each of the legs down to the cuff." Relieved, I selected the iridescent mustard color over the bilious green and the dutch boy blue. Izzy carefully marked the pants for alterations and stated that the pants would be ready Saturday. I left Izzy to hitch hike home, eagerly anticipating my return and my new image.

On Saturday, I got up early, dressed and again hitch hiked to Izzy's store. Izzy greeted me like an old friend, calling me by name and complementing me on my blue suede shoes. He retrieved my iridescent mustard pants from the tailor shop and showed me to a dressing room. I had to tug and pull to get my feet through the narrow openings at the bottom. After the pants were on, I put on my blue suede shoes and left the dressing room in search of the three sided mirror I had noticed on the previous visit. Looking into the mirror, I smiled. These pants were just what I wanted, and they were a perfect fit.

I left Izzy and caught a ride with an old farmer, driving what seemed to be an even older pick-up truck. The farmer was wearing bib overalls and a straw farm hat. Tobacco juice dribbled down his chin as he spit out of the driver's side window every half mile or so. In the course of conversation, I showed the old man my new pants, thinking to impress him. "Kinda bright, ain't they," was his only reply. I sat in silence for the rest of the trip, realizing that the old man had no sense of fashion.

The next morning, I dressed for church. I, of course, put on my new iridescent mustard color pants, and my blue suede shoes, followed by a white shirt and a hand painted tie, discarded by my older brother when he left home to fight in the Great War. Try as I may, I cannot clearly recall the tie, except that it was brown and blue with some object d'art emblazoned between the knot and the lower tip. Then I put on a brown and white houndstooth sport coat (my only sport coat), which was at least a half size too small. I wasn't completely satisfied with the look, but what the heck, this was the new style.

As I left for church, my mother gave me a rather stupid look. Her mouth was wide open and she just stared at me, as if she had just seen a ghost. No matter. She would just have to get used to the new me.

On my way to church, I had to cross a long river bridge connecting the two sides of my hometown. The bridge was an old concrete bridge with a sidewalk on both sides and a center area for vehicular travel, barely wide enough for two cars to pass. I was about half way across the bridge when a car driven by a man, probably in his early thirties, with his wife and two young children, slowly passed me. The man looked in my direction, shook his head from side to side and said, "Look at that God damned clown!" The wife had the same look my mother had when I left the house. The grimy little children with their food encrusted faces just stared.

Visibly shaken, I walked another ten feet and then turned, tracing my steps to the safety and solitude of my home. At home, I quickly changed clothes, mumbling every obscenity within my vocabulary. I didn't go to church that day. I just couldn't deal with God and the iridescent mustard colored pants on the same day.

I never, ever wore my West Coast pants again. My home town just wasn't ready for high fashion.

NO MORE YEAS

Every time a baby is born in a coal mining town, the doctor amputates one arm or gouges out one eye so that the child won't grow up self conscious. That's callous, sick humor, you say. Well, wake up and meet reality. The mines and mining towns epitomize the lowest depths of human degradation in these United States, marking the land that God and the U.S. Government forgot. This was so in the early fifties. Today, it is much worse.

When I was playing high school football in the early fifties, I dreaded traveling to the mining towns to play football. No one talked much about it, but I knew that my team mates harbored the same feelings. Although we routinely won the ball games, something bad was sure to occur either during, before or after the game.

One year, while traveling the winding mountain roads to Meadow Bridge, West Virginia, for a football game, I had a rather eerie feeling. We always traveled to out of town games in private cars, forming a caravan, probably for safety. Unlike most of our trips, no one spoke. The sky was a black overcast, giving the appearance that the dark clouds were trying to swallow the surrounding mountains. Added to the dreary atmosphere was the fact that Meadow Bridge had an exceptionally good football team with huge linemen, fast running backs and a better than average quarterback—the offspring of those who go deep into the belly of the earth, risking life and limb on a daily basis, just to earn a living.

As we neared Meadow Bridge, the rough, wood cabins in carved out areas on the sides of mountains and the dirty little children playing along the edge of the road, throwing coal or rocks at the passing cars, added to my feelings of morbidity. Then, at the edge of town, we saw the coal tipple, used to load coal onto trucks and railroad cars. This was the final blow, for I have yet to see a coal tipple without thinking of those men working in cramped spaces deep beneath the earth, sometimes with restricted air and light, in order to extricate lumps of coal, called Appalachian gold by the State's politicians—the singular product with the most economic impact on those who live in the Appalachian mountains.

At the high school, we dressed quickly and took the field. I, for one, was anxious to get this game over with, win or lose. The pregame warm up was the longest I ever experienced. Before the game started, I was able to "suck it up" and focus on the game ahead and the opposing player.

My opponent was, indeed big, outweighing me by more than thirty pounds, with a couple of teeth missing, a few days growth of beard and an ugly scowl, obviously created to intimidate me. But, I was able to sublimate the image before me, remembering my instructions, "hit low, hard and quick." This proved to be my salvation, for my opponent was slow and after a few plays he began to back up when the ball was snapped. Thereafter, size didn't matter and I could do anything I wanted with "Big Ugly."

There were several plays, however, when old Ugly either didn't fall all the way to the ground or was able to get up quicker than I anticipated. On those plays, I paid the price. He would jump on my back and stomp several times before the play ended. After the game, I discovered that my back was bleeding from neck to waist.

During the latter part of the third quarter, Ugly snorted, "You sons-a-bitches may win the game, but you ain't goin to win the fight afterwards." Somehow, I believed him.

In the fourth quarter, I thought hail was falling. I could hear it hitting my helmet but I couldn't see any signs of hail on the ground. At the same time, I experienced a stinging sensation on my face. I was confused. Then, I looked toward the opponent's sidelines and saw ten to fifteen kids throwing slate.

We won the game handily. Afterwards, we quickly gathered our clothes and surrounded by our townspeople, the local police and the West Virginia Highway Patrol, made our way to our caravan. We left Meadow Bridge with a police escort, happy with our win and happy to be alive.

Back in our home town, we learned the fate of our Methodist preacher. Now to begin with, this particular preacher was himself an oddity. He was always dressed in a suit and tie and wore a homburg hat, looking as out of place in the mountains of West Virginia as a mountain man with gallous overalls would look on Wall Street. He was sometimes referred to as the Bishop or the High Priest by the other ministers in town.

According to reports, the preacher, sitting on the top row of the visitor's bleachers, jumped up at one point in the early part of the game and yelled, "Yea, Alderson!" He was immediately hit in the face by a miner, causing him to fall off the back side of the bleachers to the ground, a distance of maybe ten feet, resulting in a fractured arm. The miner looked around at the visiting crowd and calmly announced, "There'll be no more yeas." And, for the remainder of this particular game, there were, in fact, no more yeas.

Over the years, I have driven through the mining country a number of times. Now, mobile homes with satellite dishes (the state tree of West Virginia) dot the landscape, but the poverty of the people remains. The miners have been used by the mine owners, the unions and the politicians—raped and violated, if you will—and discarded to live off the land like their forefathers. They live without hope or expectation, for themselves or for their children. They are, indeed, the lost tribe. At the same time, the large coal removing equipment decapitates mountain after mountain, leaving in their wake complete destruction of the environment. Looking at the destruction of those beautiful mountains and the people who live there, the thought returns, "There are no more yeas."

WIRE'S BIG DATE

"He couldn't make out in a whorehouse with a fist full of thousands." That remark was invariably heard every time Wire, one of the legends of Alderson, West Virginia, walked away from the "end of the bridge," the gathering place for most of the young men in my home town.

Wire was probably in his early forties, although his appearance suggested that he might be much older. He had a rather gaunt look, indicative of too much alcohol and too little food—a look evidently acquired during or after one of his trips to Detroit (pronounced Dee-troit) where he worked on an assembly line, patiently waiting for an injury or to be laid off. In either case he could return home to draw his "rockin chair," a term generally used to describe disability or unemployment benefits.

At the end of the bridge, one of the boys said that Wire's heavy drinking started after a waitress in Detroit told him, "Wire, honey, I can't go to bed with you. My body would never forgive me." There was probably no truth to the story, but it did add to Wire's legend.

Wire was about 5' 6" in height, weighed maybe 120 pounds and walked with a distinct stumbling swagger, which became more and more pronounced depending on whether he was drinking, drunk, blind drunk or blind, running drunk. His facial scars were monuments to lost fights in virtually every beer joint within his range of travel. He had no teeth and when he spoke his lips flapped sending spit in several directions at the same time. As a result, there was always a distance of five feet or more between Wire and his audience.

His running buddy was a fellow named Axe Head, Wire's mirror image, except for teeth. Axe Head did have teeth. Together Wire and Ax Head were down right surly, especially when their blood alcohol level exceeded .15, which was all too often. They took offense at almost every comment or every gesture and loudly cursed and threatened everyone within hearing distance.

Although we were all aware that Wire and Axe Head could be dangerous, most of us at the end of the bridge were highly entertained with these two miniatures—strutting, cursing and threatening—looking like some sort of caricatures. They always left after a short time in search of more wine, beer or whiskey, or a combination thereof, and to my knowledge, no one was ever injured at the end of the bridge by either Wire or Axe Head.

Actually, I always suspected that Wire and Axe Head never lingered long at the end of the bridge because Wire considered this particular place a sort of Holy ground. After all, he was a frequent guest lecturer at the end of the bridge, speaking about sex and women, recounting his sexual exploits as if he were Don Juan and intimating that all of the women in town were mesmerized by his charm and good looks.

We were all aware that there was little truth in any of Wire's stories; yet, each story changed with every new telling—so much so that several minutes would pass before anyone realized he was listening to one of Wire's old stories. Then too, the thought of Wire as a lothario was, in and of itself, amusing. So, we tolerated Wire and his stories as a part of our entertainment at the end of the bridge.

Wire told several stories about the loss of his false teeth. The one I liked best involved a woman Wire was seeing in Detroit. Wire, flush with the new money from his employment, took his lady friend to one of Detroit's better restaurants, ordered hors d'oeuvres (pronounced by Wire as whores de ovaries), steaks with all the trimmings and two bottles of the best house wine, a fine Lambrusco imported all the way from California with the "screw off cap." Wire noticed that his lady friend was having difficulty eating her steak. She had no teeth. Being the true gentleman that he was, Wire offered his teeth, a gesture readily accepted by his girl friend. According to Wire, the lady ate her steak without difficulty and remarked that Wire's teeth were an exceptionally good fit. As the night progressed, both got blind running drunk and Wire woke up the next morning in his car, with limited memory of the night before. Unfortunately, Wire never saw his lady friend or his teeth after that night. It was a good story, but everyone knew that the story was a lie. Or, was it?

Then it happened. One of the younger guys said, "That's a damned lie, Wire. You couldn't make out in a whorehouse with a fist full of thousands." There was a hushed silence, waiting for Wire to explode and wondering about what sort of violence Wire would try to inflict on the young man. Against my better judgment, I walked to a point between Wire and the younger fellow and waited, looking for Wire to pull a knife or lash out with his fists. Wire's reaction was totally unexpected. He simply hung his head, like a little boy caught with his hand in the cookie jar, turned and walked toward his car.

Thereafter, Wire was not seen nor heard from for more than two weeks—not at the end of the bridge, not at the pool room, not at Mack's Snack Shack and not at any of the several beer joints which formed his regular circuit. All of us at the end of the bridge were concerned—particularly concerned that Wire, stripped of all of his rationalizations, might resort to suicide.

Finally, after much worry and unwarranted concern, I saw Wire's old car weaving toward a parking spot at the service station directly across from the end of the bridge. The driver's door opened and Wire's ugly yellow dog emerged. Four or five of us began walking toward the car when Wire leaned out of the driver's window and said, "You bastards feed Dog while I'm gone." At once we knew that Wire was not just drunk, but blind running drunk. When we reached the car, we could see Rosie sitting in the front passenger seat with her dress hiked up to her waist, with no panties and with a broad smile on her face. She, too, was blind running drunk.

The back seat of the car was filled with three cases of beer, cans of sardines and several bags of assorted groceries. Wire announced that he and Rosie were going camping and that they would return

Sunday night for Dog. The old car sped away and we all watched the tail lights moving from one lane to the other until the car was out of sight.

Laughter rang out that night at the end of the bridge, as each of us recounted the recent events. Of course, Wire had set out to prove that he could, indeed, attract a woman and that he didn't need a " fist full of thousands" to do so. The event was planned by Wire and carried out to perfection. He wanted several of the boys at the end of the bridge to see Rosie, totally exposed, leaving for an entire weekend of sexual delights with Wire.

The plan was excellent, with one exception. Wire used the wrong woman to restore his reputation. Like Wire, Rosie could always be found in some state of drunkenness, usually at one of the beer joints in town, eventually leaving (if she was lucky) with one or more of the customers who had become drunk enough to appreciate her beauty. Only a few men in the immediate area ever reached this state of drunken euphoria. Every one of us at the end of the bridge knew Rosie. She lived on the Mountain, seven or eight miles from town. She had no means of transportation and little, if any, money; yet, Rosie managed to spend each Friday and Saturday night at one of the beer joints until closing time, unless sooner incarcerated for public drunkenness, which occurred with some frequency.

In any event, Saturday and Sunday, until the early evening, were terrible. It rained the better part of both days, a windswept downpour of steady rain, and everyone who had sense enough to get out of the rain, did. The rain ceased shortly before dusk on Sunday. Wire and Rosie arrived a short time later to the cheers of a waiting crowd, gathered at the end of the bridge to memorialize the event.

It was obvious that Wire was in no mood to be social. From the car window he shouted, "You bastards stay over there and don't mess with me." We did as he said. After all, two full days and nights with Rosie inside of a car in a pouring rain was beyond our individual or collective imagination.

Wire yelled for his dog. The old yellow dog came from out of nowhere and ran up to the driver's side of the car, wagging his tail in eagerness to see his master. Wire opened the driver's door. The dog stopped short of jumping into Wire's lap to sniff the interior of the car, then stepped back a couple of steps and let out a howl that could be heard blocks away. Still howling, Dog ran away from the car toward the pool room. The smells of Wire, Rosie, the beer and the sardines were not what Dog expected. It was several days before Wire was able to coax Dog back to the car.

In the end, Wire had his big date, which proved nothing to the boys at the end of the bridge, but in the process, he damned near lost his dog. Wire never wanted to talk about his date with Rosie and his big weekend. We obliged, at least in Wire's presence, for none of us could think of anything worse in life than spending two days and nights inside a car with Rosie, in a rain storm, and almost losing your faithful dog at the same time.

GHOSTS IN THE
REAR VIEW MIRROR

A stranger, dressed in well worn army fatigues and combat boots, emerged from the ESSO service station at the end of the bridge, directly across the road from the billboard sign. His boots were badly scuffed, and his fatigues, spotted with food stains, grease and dirt, together with his matted long hair and unruly beard, gave the stranger an air of mystery. I guessed that he was a veteran of World War II who, like many of his brother soldiers, had never become acclimated to civilian life. He probably lived deep in the mountains, in a small cabin with a couple of old hound dogs. There was little doubt that the stranger was unmarried or that he was regularly employed. At least, this was my reasoning.

The stranger got into a vintage pick up truck, with West Virginia license plates, and no bumpers, marked with dusty, red-orange primer, separated by patches of what appeared to be the original green paint. Obviously, the truck was held together with baling wire and bondo, not unlike many trucks in the area. I smiled, thinking, "West Virginia camouflage."

The man made a wide U-turn, passing directly in front of the sign board. I could hear his laugh through the open passenger window as he waved to the boys at the end of the bridge. In the rear window of the truck there was a hand-made sign which read, "NONCONFORMISTS ARE ALL ALIKE."

I thought about those words for several minutes, but I just couldn't seem to grasp the meaning. I considered myself to be a nonconformist—a unique person, unlike any other person; and, I knew that most of my friends, especially the boys at the end of the bridge were nonconformists, unwilling to accept the rules and regulations established by our parents' generation. We were destined to form the new age—the new world, if you will. After all, it was 1951.

Maybe the stranger was referring to himself. But, if so, why did he laugh as he drove past the end of the bridge. The subtle meaning was more than my young mind could grasp.

The boys at the end of the bridge were, indeed, nonconformists. Everyone in town said so. We all wore tight legged jeans, white or grey t-shirts, white athletic socks and penny loafers or blue suede shoes. The hair cut was either a flat top or duck tails, kept in place by some variety of wax or greasy hair formula.

In the left rear pocket of the blue jeans was a brown or black billfold, with two or three dollars (never more than ten dollars), perhaps the picture of a girl friend, and most certainly a condom, which over time left an unmistakable imprint on the outside of the billfold.

The most acceptable brand of condom was "Sheik" or "Trojan," neither of which conjures up anything akin to love or sexual pleasure, a likely reason why most of my generation and those before had such misconceptions about women and sex.

And, most importantly, almost all of the boys over the age of sixteen possessed a West Virginia driver's license, prominently displayed under a plastic window on the inside of the billfold. Unfortunately, I was one of those who fell into the almost category. I was sixteen years, one month and two days old, without much hope of ever obtaining a driver's license.

My father and mother never owned a car, nor had a driver's license. Neither did my two sisters. My brother, who lived out of state, had just gotten his license, after four years in military service and four more years of college, but he was of no help.

Before he died, my father frequently said, with complete sincerity, "There's no place I can think of that I might ever want to go that I can't get to by walking or riding a train," a statement often repeated by my mother, most particularly when I made mention of a car or a driver's license.

I was completely perplexed. I could think of no one who would teach me to drive a car, much less use that car to take the test for the driver's license. Besides, I didn't have the assurance that I could master shifting gears with the use of a clutch, considering the time constraints for anyone fool enough to teach me to drive a car.

While several of my friends were already driving, they were all driving their parent's car or truck. Accordingly, I could not conceive that any one of those friends would risk damage to the family vehicle by allowing me to take the wheel of what was most certainly one of the family's prized possessions, even though the vehicle might be several years old.

All of this might be difficult to comprehend for those who were not raised in the '40s or '50s. Today almost everyone has an automobile, even many teenagers below the driving age, but in the '50s, the family automobile or sometimes the family truck was just that—a family vehicle purchased and maintained for the entire family; and, it was a rarity when any family, at least in southern West Virginia, had more than one vehicle.

Just when I thought I had considered all of my options, I had a true epiphany—if you will, a message from God, who, from a multiplicity of prayers, was well aware of my problem. The name "Hallie Jones" popped into my brain, after which everything became crystal clear.

Hallie was an elementary school teacher by profession, but her true love was music, which should have been her vocation, for she had one of the most beautiful operatic soprano voices I have ever heard. And, I sang bass in the Old Greenbrier Baptist Church choir, directed by Hallie Jones.

A rather impressive figure, with her high heeled shoes, which she always wore, Hallie was at least six feet tall, which was most unusual for women of that day. Her ample breasts made her appear much larger and her direct approach to almost everything, intimidated most men, which was probably the reason she had not married. Yet, I always had the feeling that Hallie and I might have become more than just friends, if it were not for the fifteen to twenty years difference in our ages.

But, there was another reason why Hallie was the perfect person to assist me in my quest for a driver's license. She owned a new Chevrolet coupe, with an automatic transmission. No shifting gears. No clutch. "I will have no trouble driving this car," I thought. After all, I had watched others driving a car, and use of the steering wheel or the brake pedal seemed to be the least of their problems.

After Hallie was selected as my driving mentor, I spent several days formulating my plan. When approaching Hallie, should I be candid and confess that I had never driven a car? Should I ask her to teach me to drive or simply ask her to take me to Union, West Virginia, where the driver's test was given? What would be my approach? And, how would I overcome her objections?

I finally convinced myself that I had nothing to lose—that Hallie's rejection would leave me in no worse position than I was in at the time. So, armed with the faux bravery peculiar to teenage males, I walked to Hallie's house, oblivious of the fact that only a complete fool would grant my request, without inquiry or objections.

Hallie answered the door with a smile and welcomed me into her home. I was so nervous I was shaking, at least inside, if not outwardly, and everything within me seemed to be lodged in my throat, choking off my words. Finally, after mumbling for several minutes, I blurted, "Hallie, would you take me to Union for my driver's test?"

To my surprise, she said, without hesitation, "I would be pleased and honored to take you for your driver's test. When do you want to go?" *What?* No objections? No questions? No reservations?

Friday was the best day for Hallie, four days away. Hallie smiled again and I mumbled, "Thank you," as I left my newest, best friend's house, walking, with a bouncy step, toward the end of the bridge. I was elated. No, I was more than elated. In four days I would have my West Virginia driver's license.

The next three days proved to be the most intense days of my life. Could I drive Hallie's car? Would I make any mistakes in the presence of the Highway Patrolman? Would I fail the driver's test? I didn't sleep much, and I found myself quiet and pensive in the presence of my family and friends, none of whom were aware of my plans.

I met Hallie at her home at exactly 1:30 p.m. on Friday. I noticed that Hallie had backed the Chevrolet into her driveway, which meant that I would simply need to start the car, turn left onto North Monroe Street, then drive straight to Union. While this was true, I would still have to drive across a bridge barely wide enough for two cars to pass, and at the end of South Monroe Street, I would have to drive up the mountain, around curves that were hazardous under the best of conditions.

As anticipated, Hallie asked me to drive. I started the engine, shifted into drive, and after stopping at the end of the driveway, turned left onto North Monroe Street toward the bridge. Two approaching cars passed and the drivers waved, as was the custom. I concentrated on my driving, hoping that there would be no cars on the bridge. To my relief, there were no other cars on the bridge, and I continued toward my next obstacle—the mountain.

I had walked the mountain road many times and generally knew the contour of the curves. The road was built or rebuilt in the '30s by the WPA, a government agency which employed workers for public projects in an effort to stimulate the economy during the depression years. My brother-in-law claimed that he always knew when a road had been constructed or reconstructed by the WPA. He said, "The WPA takes a straight stretch of road, puts in four or five sharp curves, then banks those curves in such a way that the road becomes an immediate hazard." This mountain road was no exception.

I passed the Chevrolet Garage on my left, with the incline approaching, and slowed the car to a snail's pace, when I heard Hallie say, "Speed up or we'll never get to Union. I pressed down on the accelerator going into the first curve, but quickly applied the brakes when I began to lose control of the car. I moved straight into each curve, which resulted in a sharp move to square off the curve. On the last curve, I glanced over at Hallie. All of the blood had drained from her face, and her mouth was open wide. She was speechless.

When I reached the top of the mountain, I knew that the worst of the trip was over. While there were other curves en route to Union, the mountain curves were the most treacherous. Accordingly, my confidence built for the remainder of the trip.

Finally we arrived in Union, found the Highway Patrol Station, and I successfully parked the Chevrolet in an angular parking space, with no other vehicles parked in the spaces either to my right or to my left. I noticed that there didn't seem to be any parallel parking spaces in the small town of Union, for which I was eternally grateful.

After breezing through the written exam, the Highway Patrolman said in a loud, gruff voice, "Let's drive." He and I got into Hallie's car, leaving Hallie in the patrol station, relieved, I am sure, that she would not be riding with us.

The Patrolman's first question threw me for a loop. He barked, "Have you checked your emergency brake?" I had seen some of my friends setting the emergency brake on their cars or trucks with the left foot, although I had never bothered to discover exactly where the emergency brake was located, how it was set or how it was released. I looked to my left, below the dash and saw nothing that looked like an emergency brake. Then, I opened the driver's door, got out of the car, and bending over, looked under the dash. Again, no sign of an emergency brake. I got back into the car and responded, "This is the first time I have driven this car and I don't think it has an emergency brake." The Patrolman rolled his eyes, mumbled something and pointed to a handle to my right, under the dash, directly below the radio. "That's the emergency brake; now, let's go," he said.

I backed out of the parking space and drove straight ahead, waiting for my instructions, before reaching a stop sign. I came to a gradual stop, whereupon the Officer directed me to turn right. I was almost petrified at this point. Instead of turning right, I turned left.

The Patrolman almost shouted, "How in the hell can I give a driver's test, when you don't know your left from your right?" As I apologized, I could feel my face turn beet red from embarrassment.

I could tell that my left turn had confused the Patrolman. This route was not in his plan. In disgust, he told me to keep turning left until we arrived back at the Patrol Station. In my best effort to please, I turned left into an alley, drove to the next block, again turned left and made my way back to the Patrol Station. About thirty feet from the Patrol Station, the Officer pointed to a parking space between two parked vehicles and said, "Whip in here?" Whip I did. I turned into the parking space, stomping on the brake pedal after I had moved several feet into the parking space. The Patrolman was thrown against the dash and windshield. His hat came off and landed on the floorboard. His clipboard was found in the back seat.

It took the Patrolman and I several seconds to regain our composure, after which we got out of the car and walked on unsteady legs to his office. Inside the office, with the door closed, he began to speak. His voice appeared to be almost an octave higher than when I first heart him speak. Also, there was a stutter in his speech, which I had not noticed before. I was sure I was going to hyperventilate for the first time in my life.

The Patrolman began to speak, "You di-di-did re-re-real ba-ad. I-I wa-want yo-ou to pr-promise m-m-me that (after a few moments to regain his composure, the stuttering disappeared) ah-ah-ah you will practice driving a car in a ten acre field for at least two or three weeks before you ever drive on the roads of West Virginia." What else could I do? I promised.

Then, came the surprise. The Patrolman said, "Against my better judgment, I'm going to give you your driver's license. If you want a reason, I will tell you that I never, ever want to get into a car with you again. That's my reason."

I left the office overjoyed and, at the same time, despondent. I had my driver's license to display in my billfold along with my condom; yet, I knew that I was not ready to drive a car.

I could see the surprise in Hallie's eyes when I told her that I had passed the driver's test. She smiled and said, "Let me have the keys. You've had a long stressful day." With a sigh of relief, I handed the keys to Hallie for the ride home.

To my knowledge, Hallie never repeated the events of that day to anyone. Moreover, more than ten years passed before I related those events to my wife, when she was teaching me to drive a car with a manual transmission.

Over the years, I get a lump in my throat and mild nausea, every time I see a police car in my rear view mirror. You see, I am convinced that every policeman knows—they *all* know—that I never practiced driving in a ten acre field before I started driving on the West Virginia highways.

CRINOLINE AND PLAYTEX

The scourge of every virile young man in the late forties and early fifties had to be the crinoline underskirt. Made of cotton or horsehair or perhaps a combination thereof, stiffened by some process known only to engineers and mothers and layered with several layers of the God awful fabric in a kind of maze, the crinoline underskirt was worn under a full skirt to form a bell shape from the waist to the end of the skirt. The poodle skirt was incomplete without the crinoline underskirt, bobby sox and penny loafers. Sometimes, a skirt with the crinoline under-skirt would be worn without hose or socks, topped by a sweater or blouse and the standard double cone bra. This outfit, particularly on blondes with pigtails, always left me with the feeling that the girl was about to yodel.

And, a young woman wearing crinoline was certain to be wearing a playtex girdle. Some sadistic advertising genius probably coined the name, because there would be no play for Tex when the woman was wearing this girdle.

My confrontations with the playtex girdle were generally in times of darkness. Therefor, I have no notion of what the girdle looked like, but the feel was unmistakable; it felt like rubber molded to the body—a virtual chastity belt, requiring the undivided attention of at least two people, or maybe a device akin to a shoe horn, for removal. If you ever wondered why there were so few unwanted pregnancies in the forties and fifties, I can direct you, without reservation, to the crinoline underskirt and the playtex girdle.

A date in the late forties and early fifties would go something like this. I would walk to the girl's house and knock on the front door. After a respectable time, the door would open wide, and there, standing in front of me, with a half smile, would be my date accompanied by her mother whose broad smile, just short of outright laughter, told me in no uncertain terms, "You ain't going to score tonight."

My girl and I would then walk to the theater, as planned, holding hands and engrossed in meaningless chatter—usually local gossip. Approaching the bridge which joined the side of town where my girlfriend lived to the theater side, we both changed our demeanor. I knew that the cat calls from the boys at the end of the bridge would be embarrassing; so I dropped her hand until we were well onto the bridge. She understood.

In the theater, there would be a light touch of shoulder, breast or leg—nothing really overt, since the hair on the back of my neck told me that a dozen eyes were watching. I would stare at the movie screen, totally oblivious of the movie being shown. In my head, a thousand little vaginas would be swimming, in, out and around whatever mental faculties I had left, hungry for the movie to end.

At the movie's end, we would begin the slow, deliberate walk back to my girl's home, stopping from time to time in the darkened areas to kiss and fondle, until we reached the place of detour to our favorite spot, a secret place which shall remain secret, even after all these years. There, I would begin groping in earnest, making my way through the layers of crinoline to the sacred areas covered by the playtex—the impenetrable fortress covering her womanhood.

Like a warrior general, I tried to enter the fortress at several locations, all without success. Finally, I concluded that the best approach would be to try removing the girdle by taking a firm hold on the waistband and pulling downward. The theory seemed sound; however, the act of removing the girdle was another matter. You see, I had one arm around my girlfriend's waist, leaving only one arm for the task at hand. Moreover, we were kissing. Earlier, I had learned that if you don't keep one arm around the girl's waist and continue kissing, the spell is broken. A girl has visions of pregnancy, shotgun weddings and complete loss of reputation and runs home in a fit of anger. As a result, I kept one arm around her waist and continued kissing. This left a great deal to be desired, for in the darkness, I was like a blind man with one arm.

Suddenly, I had a sense of hope. I almost shouted. With great effort and dexterity, I was finally able to move the left side down two or three inches. I immediately began working on the right side. After pulling the right side down a couple of inches, I went back to the left side only to find that the left side had moved back to the waist.

But, time was my enemy. With no forewarning, my girl shoved me away, looked at her watch and exclaimed, "Oh no, it's 11:00 o'clock!" Her curfew was 11:00 p.m. We quickly got up and ran to her front porch where she gave me a hurried kiss and quickly entered the house, leaving me in a state of total confusion. Walking home, my legs were like rubber. My skin was clammy. My head was pounding, probably from the swimming vaginas, and my testicles ached like a tooth ache. In a few short hours I had undergone a strange metamorphosis—from gentility to raging bull to amoebae. I was a rag.

These scenes were reenacted time and again throughout the late forties and early fifties, to the delight of parents and to the consternation of young men, throughout the nation. Ultimately, the sexual revolution, marked the end of crinoline and playtex. Now, crinoline underskirts are only worn by square dancers. I suspect playtex girdles are gone forever.

Today, we are all concerned with sexual promiscuity, teen age pregnancy and aids. Solutions range from total abstinence to "just say no" to introducing kindergartners to condoms. Everyone, it seems, has thoughts, with no definitive answers.

Has no one ever considered crinoline and playtex?

PARROT

It wasn't so much that he didn't bathe regularly or that he had a surly look or even that he appeared oblivious to civilized society which piquet the anger and disgust of the entire town. In fact, Parrot didn't bathe at all. He was surly. And, he didn't give a damn about civilized society. As a result, civilized society turned it's back on the man they called Parrot.

No one, it seems, remembered much about Parrot's early life. His parents either died young or they became so embittered at having produced such a child that they left, never to return. Some claimed that he was raised, if you can call it that, by a hermit uncle who died when Parrot was in his teens. Formal schooling was out of the question, and the informal education received from the old uncle consisted of learning to trap small animals or to harvest berries and roots for food, particularly ramps—an onion-like root which left a repugnant odor that lasted for days—learning to make a fire using flintstone, and learning all of the other survival skills known by our forgotten ancestors and discarded by civilized society.

Others claimed that Parrot was raised in a good household, graduated from high school, married and worked on the C&O Railroad until his wife pissed him off and he retired at an early age.

In any case, Parrot's home, with or without a wife and family, was in the woods near a small community known as Wolf Creek, five or six miles from the nearest civilized town—my home town. During my young lifetime, Parrot never worked and never received any governmental assistance; and while the country was in the midst of the war to end all wars, Parrot was not called to serve. Quite likely, the government never knew he existed. It's probably just as well, for this strange mountain man would have been as much a leper in the military as he was in civilized society.

Although he would always be ostracized from polite society—actually from any kind of society—Parrot was forever drawn to the streets and the stores, the motorized vehicles and the general hustle and bustle of my home town, particularly on Saturdays when the streets were crowded with miners and sawmill workers, visiting or home for the weekend, generally content to spend the day at one or more of the three beer joints on Railroad Avenue, across from the train station.

And so, Parrot would come to town almost every Saturday—not to shop or talk—but just to stand at the street corner in front of the bank, watching everyone and everything. The dark, piercing eyes were, at times frightening, at other times pitiful. He reminded me of a cur dog, reacting from years of being beaten and kicked, not knowing whether to lay down and whimper or attack.

My mother gave me strict orders to stay away from Parrot. As a boy of five or six, this only aroused my interest. My parents owned and operated a "mom and pop" restaurant, a block from the bank. Working twelve or more hours each day, except Sunday, they had little time to attend to a young boy, with too much energy and too little fear. The streets and stores were my playground and I knew all of the merchants and their employees, as well as the local policeman. Why, then, should I be scared of a scruffy looking mountain man that smelled like a goat? He wouldn't dare hurt me with all of my close friends nearby.

So, I walked right up to Parrot, stared him square in the eye and told him my name. He only grunted. Then I said, "Why do they call you Parrot? That's a bird."

"Don't know," he replied. I turned and proudly walked home, thinking that my first conversation with the mountain man had gone quite well.

Although Parrot had no visible source of income, he always had a little money, likely from harvesting and selling ginseng, which was considered as a powerful aphrodisiac, even during the early forties. That money was mostly spent on beer, Parrot's only luxury and his greatest downfall.

Parrot would arrive in town almost every Saturday, early in the morning before the stores opened. For many years, he rode on the flatbed of a truck owned by his neighbors, the Fanchers. Old man Fancher and his wife walked the streets from the time the stores opened until almost noon when they would get back into their old truck and drive home, leaving Parrot to walk the five or six miles back to his mountain shack. It was only then that Parrot would buy his quart of beer from the rear entrance of one of the beer joints. (None of the business establishments allowed Parrot to grace their premises.)

Then one Saturday, Mrs. Fancher, who always walked ten paces or so behind her husband, became preoccupied and failed to see her husband stop to speak to a neighbor. Without knowing it, she walked a few steps in front of Mr. Fancher. This was the last time Mrs. Fancher was ever seen in town. Thereafter, Mr. Fancher would come to town intermittently to buy seed or groceries. But the regular Saturday trips ceased, and along with them, Parrot's transportation.

Since no one else ever gave Parrot a ride, he walked to town, arriving a little later in the day. And, he also started drinking earlier. It was an accepted fact that Parrot couldn't handle strong drink. With the Fanchers no longer present, he would usually be drunk before noon and spend the remainder of the day in a drunken stupor. In his drunkenness, he wandered the streets, with his fly open, leaving him totally exposed, since he never saw the need for underwear. This was, so to speak, the straw that broke the camel's back. The keen sensibilities of the ladies in town, including my mother, were highly offended.

One Saturday, as I walked to the grocery store with my mother (a most unusual activity for me), I spotted Parrot sitting on the sidewalk with his back against a telephone pole. He was semi-conscious and his fly was gaped open. I tugged on my mother's arm and exclaimed, in a rather loud voice, "Mom, Mom, look at Parrot's teetie winker!" Laughter exploded from a group of men nearby, which added to my mother's embarrassment. She jerked my arm so hard that I felt a lingering pain for days. We turned around and scurried back home.

A few weeks later there was a meeting of the town merchants and plans were made to take care of the "Parrot" problem. They all reasoned that if Parrot were cleaned up and fitted with new clothes he might become more civilized. At the end, a detailed plan was formulated for the civilization of Parrot.

It was a fairly warm, Spring day. Arriving at about 9:00 a.m., as anticipated, Parrot was cornered by three large men, hired by the merchants, and escorted to the back yard of a local business. His mournful sounds were heard several blocks away. He struggled for a time, then sort of went limp, realizing that his efforts were futile and that he was at the mercy of the townspeople. There, he was stripped of all of his clothing and placed in a metal tub filled with lukewarm water where he was scrubbed from head to toe with soap and coarse bristled brushes. They worked like missionaries, girded by righteousness and intent upon saving the soul of this lost, misguided heathen. Afterward, his hair and beard were trimmed by one of the local barbers and he was fitted with new clothes and boots, supplied by the local men's store. Parrot, for once in his life, appeared civilized. The merchants were generally pleased with the transformation—all except my father who refused to be a part of the plan, calling it barbaric.

A crowd gathered to watch and await the transformation from mountain man to civilized man. Everyone was in awe, for the new Parrot bore no resemblance to the Parrot they had known. When fully dressed, Parrot slowly walked to the edge of the crowd, then bolted—running for his life to the comfort and solitude of his mountain home.

A few weeks later, Parrot was found dead, still wearing the new clothing and boots provided by the townspeople. His death certificate read, "Died of natural causes." His passing didn't make the obituaries and no one could find a tombstone or other marker for his grave. Moreover, no one in town mentioned his name. It was almost as though Parrot had never lived.

Residents of Wolf Creek claim that on a clear night they can still hear the faint sounds of a wounded animal, maybe a wolf, coming from the area where Parrot lived—painful, mournful, whimpering sounds—sounds very much like the sounds made by Parrot on the day he was given a bath by the town missionaries.

THE BRIDGE

My imminent death was a sobering experience. I mentally reviewed my lifetime accomplishments—much more than I had any right to expect, yet insignificant when compared to my dreams. I would be remembered from time to time by family and friends, mostly on holidays, anniversaries and birthdays; then my light would slowly fade to obscurity.

The family meeting, a few days before, was sad and tearful. I expressed my eternal love for my wife and each of my children, desperately trying to say all of those things I had neglected to say during better days, knowing full well that most of my acknowledgments were too little and much too late.

My personal possessions, treasures acquired mostly through inheritance, were given to my wife and children—my father's pocket watch, three pieces of antique furniture and a Bowie knife, crafted from a wagon wheel found on the Oregon Trail. Taking stock of my life and my possessions, I was surprised that these few items of property, painstakingly made by craftsmen who obviously loved their work, were my only treasures. All of the rest—the automobiles, furniture, clothing, jewelry, computers, etc.—were insignificant. The house and bank accounts would, of course, immediately become my wife's property at the moment of my death, as well as a rather meager retirement account and two life insurance policies.

With my family in the next room mourning, I eased into my favorite chair, a blue, leather recliner, took a long, deliberate draw on my last cigarette and closed my eyes, somehow knowing that the end was at hand. I suddenly felt an ethereal rush as my soul left my body. I was eager to meet my Maker, but anxious at the thought of being confronted with my lifetime of indiscretions. Then came the shocker. Having absolutely no control over my soul, I'm being transported through a dimly lit tunnel with a bright light at the far end.

Then, I began to move more slowly, ultimately finding myself standing on a paved street facing two sets of railroad tracks. Across the tracks, to my left was an old, dilapidated two story building with a porch on both the first and second level. A rather large woman was standing on the upper porch, looking and listening for a train. I recognized this woman. She spent her entire life, each day, looking for trains and waiving to the workmen and passengers of each passing train. Everyone called her "Mama Choo-Choo."

I couldn't understand why I had such a clear vision of Mama Choo-Choo. To my recollection, I had never had a conversation with the woman, nor did I know anything about her. Maybe it was some sort of symbolism. Perhaps my life had been spent looking for the passing trains, wishing and dreaming, but never daring to take the ride.

I quickly crossed the railroad tracks. Directly in front of me was a wonderful old concrete bridge. A road, barely wide enough for two cars to pass was at the center of the bridge, flanked by a sidewalk on each side with solid concrete banisters, high enough for safety but low enough for a view of the river below.

I walked a few feet onto the bridge and looked upward. There were mountains everywhere—mountains which seemed to rise abruptly on each side of the river, with lush, green forests, intermittently punctuated by rock slopes that appeared to have been carved by a master craftsman. Unlike other mountains, these mountains were personal, each with a different name and a different personality. Like a reunion with almost forgotten friends, I savored my reunion with the mountains for what must have been several minutes, then laughed. Eternity was new to me and I couldn't yet measure time or know whether time was even measured.

I not only felt the clear, cool air that exists only in the mountains during early spring, I could actually hear, taste and smell it for the very first time, a sensation that I had totally missed during my lifetime. And, I realized that I was seeing the mountains in all of their beauty for the very first time. Experiencing the air, the mountains, the river and all of God's nature surrounding me left me with the distinct impression that I had never lived—never really lived.

The sound of voices brought me back to my after death reality. In front of me were scenes of a distant time—a time before television or computers or the internet—a time when people gathered together for the sole purpose of conversation, frequently using each other's lives and experiences for entertainment. It was a mystical time—a little like *Brigadoon*, maybe more like

Our Town or *It's A Wonderful Life*—or a strange mixture of all three.

On the sidewalks men were lifting their small children for a better view of the river or the fish swimming in the semi-clear water below. There were two young boys bent over the banister with feet dangling, looking into the water, obviously in search of fish or other aquatic life. A fisherman had just hooked a small bass, and a photographer was framing the sun's last rays on the flowing water.

Crossing the bridge, I passed friends and neighbors, in twos and threes, discussing the weather or the news of the day—some laughing, some somber. All stopped to nod or greet me as I passed. I recognized most of the people, but they all acted as though I were a stranger.

There was Neil Amold and his wife Vella, taking their evening stroll. Neil and my father were good friends as boys and continued their friendship until my father's death. My father always worried about Neil. As the story goes, Neil inherited some $10,000.00 from his parents at the end of the Depression. He immediately announced his retirement, stating that he would never do a days work for the remainder of his life.

Neil subscribed to *The Wall Street Journal* and spent his days buying and selling—stocks, commodities, real estate, futures—anything that would make money. Neil always wanted my father to join him in his various ventures, but to no avail. For my father it was too soon after the Depression; and the loss of all of his savings in a failed bank, left my father devastated—skeptical of all banks and all investments. Every time Neil would pass, my father would say,

"Poor old Neal. It's just a matter of time before he loses everything." Neil died a millionaire. My father died with a few hundred dollars, hidden in special hiding places, safe from the common thieves and the uncommon thieves at the bank.

Across the street stood Randolph Johnson, the Baptist minister, looking off into the distance, relishing the beauty of the scenery. Nearby, Coach McLaughlin was talking with a recent high school graduate and actually smiling, something he would never do while the young man was in school.

My friends and acquaintances were everywhere: Minor Bare, the sign painter, who spent more time drawing cartoons and caricatures than painting signs; Bob Watkins, a kindly old black man, disfigured in a railroad accident, who earned the respect of the entire community and who knew more about the Bible than any preacher; Jim Rowe, who served as a sort of surrogate father after my father's death; the McThenias who continually opened their house and offered their hospitality to those of us who were less fortunate and who insisted that their children, Andy and Mary Amanda, share their lives with the town's common folk; Floyd Lobban who owned the furniture store; Doc Smith who operated the local drug store and who gave me my first job at the age of fourteen (I lied about my age); Stella Nelson, the English teacher, whose dedication and insistence upon excellence was directly responsible for the future success of an inordinate number of her former students; and a host of others whose lives had directly or indirectly affected my life.

Glancing upriver I noticed my high school classmate, Harry Lee Meredith (known by everyone as Burdock), sitting in a rowboat, without paddles or oars, stationary as if anchored. His stare was transfixed on one particular mountain, looking as though he was expecting some answer.

Burdock was the only professed atheist I had ever known. His entire life had been spent in a cauldron of emotional turmoil, with one disaster followed by another. He was never really accepted—not by family and not by others. He died a tragic death. Obviously his after-life would be much like his life.

Back at the bridge, I finally saw my parents with my brother, Sheldon, and my sister, Lavinia. But, where was my sister, Ethel, and why didn't my family acknowledge my presence? Then, I realized that all of those people I had recognized had preceded me in death. My sister Ethel was still alive. For the life of me (or maybe the death), I couldn't grasp the meaning of these scenes. I shrugged and continued my journey.

At the other end of the bridge, I recognized Lute Mann's store on my right. Lute sold just about everything—cigarettes for a penny apiece, magazines, lewd comic books (kept under the counter), and a host of novelty items. Lute was virtually blind, although he was adept at handling money. As a young boy, I would enter Lute's store, speak in my deepest voice and buy anything in the store, from cigarettes to lewd comic books. I always wondered whether Lute mistook me for an older man or just didn't give a damn. I suspected that Lute knew who I was and my age. He also knew that I would be buying cigarettes and lewd books sooner or later. He reckoned that it might as well be sooner. Lute was probably right.

At the opposite corner was a sign which read, "Alderson, West Virginia—Founded in 1777 by Elder John Alderson." This was my hometown—the place where I was born and raised, from the end of the Depression years, through World War II to the middle of the Korean War.

At the end of the bridge, on my left, was a billboard sign, with a ramp or deck at the bottom, about four feet from the ground, installed for use by the billboard employees when changing billboard advertisements. There were four or five young men setting on the billboard ramp and a half dozen standing in front, telling tales of events and happenings, sometimes involving those present, but more often involving those not in attendance. It was a nightly ritual, from sundown to about midnight, and almost every young man in town, at one time or other, was a member of the "boys at the end of the bridge".

This night, the stories were familiar, relating to a semi-retarded man in town afflicted with "vocabulary dyslexia." He referred to the high school gymnasium as the gymnavy, and he claimed to have sugar diabetes so bad that it was dripping out from under his armpits. While I had heard these tales many times, I listened as one of the boys recounted the story of our mentally challenged friend saying, "If you boys don't quit bugging me, I'm going to jump off the bridge and commit adultery." During the laughter which followed, I smiled the smile of one who has told the same story dozens of times.

Watching the scene before me, I realized that I was, at one time, one of the boys at the end of the bridge, with an excellent attendance record. It was there that I acquired a love for tall tales, embellished with every telling—always told with some humor, knowing full well that the listeners, unless they were awfully dumb, could differentiate the truth from the false; and, it was there that I acquired a sense of belonging.

At this point I awoke in a cold sweat, finding myself alive and well—somewhat weakened by my experiences and with a nostalgia I had never known. After all a part of my life and my death had just passed before me. I'm told that when you die your life does, indeed, pass before you. Maybe my dream is a prelude to my death.

Afterward, I spent hours trying to interpret my dream, without much success, when I heard a small voice inside me saying, "Look upward. Look toward the mountains. Look where the air is so clear and sweet you can taste it. Look to the stories of your childhood in that small West Virginia town on the banks of the Greenbrier river, surrounded by the mountains named by your forefathers—Flat Mountain, Keeny's Knobb, Muddy Creek Mountain. Look to the boys at the end of the bridge. There you will find your answers!"

SHOES FOR SALE

World War II produced the most sweeping changes the world had ever known. Store clerks were quickly transformed into soldiers. Those with a year or two of college became pilots and navigators. Farmers from the mid-west, who had never seen the ocean, became sailors. And, men and women who, by circumstance or medical condition, were excluded from military service, served our country in the factories, mills and industries which provided the equipment, machinery and supplies for the support of our servicemen.

During those years, my brother-in-law, Denzil, worked as an electrician in the shipyards in Norfolk, Virginia, building or repairing and renovating the ships and submarines used in Naval combat and in transporting our troops to ports and small islands throughout the world. He was one of several thousands of people who migrated to this Virginia port, working ten to twelve hour shifts, sometimes six or seven days a week.

They came from all parts of the country, but mostly from Virginia, West Virginia and the Carolinas, living with their families in small row houses hurriedly constructed to accommodate the influx of new workers—all skeptical of their new jobs and their new neighbors, and ever fearful of losing the war and being enslaved by a foreign power. So, they worked and sacrificed for the good of their country. They were the unsung heros of World War II.

For the most part, the men formed their friendships with co-workers as the women and children bonded with other women and children in the neighborhood. Humor, stories of home and practical jokes were used to relieve the stress of the long hours of work and living conditions, although the housing was, for the most part, superior to their housing back home.

Those from North Carolina might declare that West Virginia, the home state of my brother-in-law, was so backward that the state tree was an outhouse. Denzil would respond by saying that those from North Carolina never wore shoes until they arrived in Norfolk. And, the kidding continued on a daily basis.

One Sunday afternoon, with nothing better to do, Denzil and my sister, Louvinia, always referred to as Beanie by her friends, assisted by their young son, Micky, made an elaborate sign which read, "One Pair of Shoes for Sale—Going Back to North Carolina." The sign was prominently displayed for more than a week in the small yard in front of Denzil and Beanie's row house, mostly for the benefit of their North Carolina friends.

Then, a strange incident happened, which was unanticipated by anyone. A clipping from a local newspaper was posted on Denzil and Beanie's front door that recited the life and the events surrounding one West Virginia family who lived in a nearby subdivision.

The family of four moved to Norfolk in the early months of 1942, persuaded that there was work at the shipyards critical to the war effort. The man was immediately hired as an apprentice welder and after three months was elevated to journeyman welder, with an appropriate increase in pay. The wife, whose skills were limited, got a job at Woolworth's 5 & 10 Cent Store, stocking shelves and waiting on customers. For the next fourteen months, she earned minimum wage, which was always taken home in cash, after she printed her name on the back side of a payroll check, as instructed by her supervisor.

The husband, in obvious emotional distress, met with the job superintendent one day and announced that he was quitting his job and that he and his family were moving back to the mountains. Not wanting to lose a good welder, the superintendent was intent upon discovering why the West Virginian suddenly wanted to leave a good job and return to the poverty he had left behind. Finally, the man said, "We just can't live on what my wife makes at Woolworth's. At least, back home I can hunt and fish and earn some money in the coal mines." After added conversation, the superintendent discovered that the West Virginian had fourteen months of uncashed payroll checks in his bureau drawer. He mistakenly believed that all of these checks could only be cashed at the end of the war.

The sign was immediately removed from Denzil and Beanie's front yard, and for the remainder of their time in Norfolk, little was mentioned about the shoeless people in North Carolina.

OLD MAN ED

He looked good in the grey, metal casket—much better than he ever looked during his lifetime. His full, silver hair was neatly trimmed and combed. His scraggly eyebrows, which always gave him a rather sinister look, were neatly plucked or trimmed and there was a conspicuous absence of hair in his nostrils and ears. The black suit formed a perfect background for the heavily starched white shirt and neatly tied tie, which appeared to choke his neck and give him a sort of chalky facade. He was downright handsome, this ninety four year old man who was referred to throughout my lifetime as Old Man Ed. He was my grandfather.

I was probably three or four years old when I first saw Old Man Ed. He came through the back door of my mother's restaurant, announced that he wanted a bowl of "God damned beans and some cornbread" and told my mother to get that boy out of his way. He smelled of body odor and beer. I had an instant dislike for this man —a dislike which persisted until his death. Over the years, I acquired a certain respect for the old man, but I never did like him. And, I suspected that the feeling was mutual.

During his early life, Old Man Ed had operated a logging camp and sawmill at various locations in the deep woods of southern West Virginia, miles from civilization. He managed to return home periodically to impregnate my grandmother, who remained at the old farm to tend the garden, milk the cows and raise the stair step children. Out of necessity, my mother left home during her early teens, moving to town to take care of an elderly woman and attend school. The ten mile walk from my mother's new home to her parental home limited visitation. As a result, my mother was never very close to her brothers and sisters, although she maintained a continuing love for her mother and a sort of supernatural respect for her father.

I don't remember much about my grandmother, except that she was a petite woman with auburn hair who was always working and who had little to say. She became seriously ill shortly after my birth and died a relatively young woman, leaving her children to the care of Old Man Ed.

Old Man Ed, to his credit, returned to the farm to make his living, raising crops, cattle and children. After the children left home, the old man sold most of the farm, retaining sufficient land for my uncle and for himself. My uncle and Old Man Ed constructed a rough one room cabin on the old man's property which Ed occupied until his death. The cabin was in a remote wooded area, at the end of a winding path leading to a graveled county road. Accordingly, I thought of my grandfather as a hermit who liked the solitude of the woods better than he liked people.

Old Man Ed's hermit status was sort of magnified by the fact that he kept a pet black snake in the cabin and a loaded double barreled shotgun next to the front door. His chin was always discolored from tobacco stains. I never saw the old man without a chew of tobacco in his mouth, except while eating. My uncle claimed that he even slept with a chew in his mouth, so that his mouth wouldn't get dry. I had never known of anyone who slept with a chew of tobacco in his mouth. These reports added to the eccentricity and the mystery of the old man.

In the late forties and early fifties squirrel hunting season was an unofficial State holiday. Many of the coal mines closed for several days out of deference to the miners, since most miners contracted a strange illness for a few days during that time of year. Armed with their prized gun, at least two bottles of whiskey and enough ammunition to eradicate the entire population of a small city, the miners took to the woods in mass. No squirrel, or for that matter cow, horse, dog or other animal, was safe. For several days each year the woods of southern West Virginia sounded like the Korean War. During those days, I was confined to the house, for the duration of the holidays.

One year, as my grandfather walked along the path to his cabin, shots rang out. Bleeding and in a half conscious state, my grandfather remembered two men standing over him. One said, "Hell, it ain't a squirrel." They left him to die.

Within a short time, my grandfather was found, apparently by other hunters and transported to the hospital. Although he was then in his early seventies and had lost a considerable amount of blood, the old man survived. He was, however, paralyzed in the left side of his body for the remainder of his life.

Old Man Ed refused to live in a nursing home or with any members of his family. So, he returned to his old cabin to remain a hermit. My uncle customized a straight chair, with casters on the legs and a board attachment which held the old man's left leg off the floor. Then, my uncle strung rope around the cabin and attached a length of rope to the bottom of the bed. Using the rope and the chair, Old Man Ed was able to move around the cabin with amazing skill, and during warm weather, he even ventured onto the porch to better commune with nature.

My aunt cooked one meal a day for the old man. He prepared the other meals for himself on the pot bellied stove. Alcohol, in any form was forbidden by the doctors. My uncle tried his best to comply with the doctor's orders, with some success, although an occasional pint of whiskey or bottle of beer would mysteriously appear. The source of the benevolence was never discovered. One day my uncle found his three small sons making "home brew" under the keen supervision of the old man. Like the beer and whiskey, the source of the fixins for the "home brew" was never discovered. The fixins were immediately destroyed and the brewery operation terminated.

This only made Old Man Ed more cantankerous. He threw all of his medicine into the pot bellied stove, referred to his doctor a "quack", and thereafter refused further medical treatment. A rather attractive woman who came to the cabin to save the old man's soul was called a whore, and probably worse. She, of course, made a rapid exit from the cabin. As word spread, visitors to the cabin became fewer and fewer until the large black snake kept under the old man's bed was his only regular companion. Many people thought Old Man Ed was crazy. Personally, I thought the old man's actions were carefully calculated to insure his peace and solitude.

But on one occasion, I, too, had reservations about the old man's mental health. The old man sent word that he wanted to see me. He heard that I was in town on holiday from the University of Tennessee in Knoxville, Tennessee. I opened the cabin door into darkness. The stench was almost unbearable. Then I heard his voice, "Come on in." The voice was almost cheerful. I never remembered hearing that voice before. As the conversation continued, the old man actually seemed interested in me.

We talked for what seemed like hours. Then, Old Man Ed disclosed that he had lived in Knoxville for a time during his youth. He directed me to a restaurant where I could get a good twenty-five cent meal with all the trimmings, and thereafter gave me the name and location of a woman I could look up if I was lonely. I left amused and perplexed. The old man finally treated me like a human being. That was the last time I saw the old man alive.

I accompanied my mother and my wife for one last look at the old man in the casket, and steered them toward the hospitality room where 1 knew all of the family members would be gathered. As we entered the room, all eyes were focused in our direction. Suddenly, one woman pointed at me and said, "See, he's the spittin image of Old Man Ed."

Another remarked, "He's more like the old man than anyone in the family." A strange look of pride settled on my mother's face.

I quickly made some excuse and retreated to a quiet area outside the funeral home. A hundred thoughts rushed through my head. I was nauseated and cold sweat covered my face. Suddenly, I had an almost over-powering urge to go off into the woods and retreat forever from civilization. Then, it dawned on me. This is exactly how Old Man Ed would have reacted.

Was the old man better than I perceived, or...? The answer still haunts me.

THE STOVE'S AH DANCIN

My father walked from the kitchen of the family restaurant to the bottom of the stairwell leading to the living area above, and loudly whispered, "Nellie, the stove's ah dancin." This was my father's daily ritual. It signaled the start of a new day for my mother and two more hours of sleep for my sister and I. Besides, my father had been up for an hour, and he needed some conversation.

My mother was already in the bathroom getting ready. She stared into the medicine cabinet mirror, carefully examining her face, especially her curved nose. Some called it a hawk nose. Nellie said it was an Indian nose. She vowed that she was part French and part Indian, a claim I never really understood, since her flawless skin, nurtured by a nightly dose of Pond's cold cream, was allergic to the sun; and, I never heard of an Indian, male or female, whose skin burned after a few minutes in the sun.

Her 5' 2" slightly plump frame, dressed in her starched white uniform appeared larger, likely the result of the one inch stack heels of her polished white shoes. Her hair that extended from head ankles had never been cut or coiffed and was never seen in its natural state by anyone except her immediate family. She carefully wrapped the strands of black, auburn and grey into a bun placed on the very top of her head and kept in place with large hair pins. The bun, which made her hair look more black than auburn or grey, was always covered with a hair net—not for any particular reason. She just liked hair nets. Now, a dusting of face powder, a touch of rouge and a little lipstick (very little) and she was ready for her long work day, a day that would end somewhere between 10:00 and 11:00 p.m.

The next day would be the same and the day after and the day after that, week in and week out, except, of course, Thanksgiving and Christmas. These were the two days she reserved for her family, but not for rest. Like every other day, Nellie cooked each holiday. The only difference was that she only cooked for her family during the holidays.

While my mother was dressing, my father had activated the coal fires in the pot belly stove in the dining room and the cook stove in the kitchen with kindling wood, (both carefully banked the night before), brewed the first pot of coffee for the day, and was preparing a breakfast for two when my mother entered the kitchen.

She immediately walked to the kitchen table and drank the concoction my father had prepared—an eight ounce glass of warm water, mixed with apple cider vinegar, a brew guaranteed by the mountain women to clean your innerds and keep you healthy. It seemed to work, since my mother was rarely sick.

She glanced toward the cook stove like a workman surveying his tools. Sure enough, the metal pad under the stove was beginning to make noises, as the stove's heat changed from warm to hot. The stove was, indeed, starting to dance.

For the next forty five minutes, my parents ate breakfast and talked. It was their time. Occasionally, I would hear the sound of my mother's laughter. She was probably laughing at some story my father heard the day before at the barbershop. Regardless, the sound of her laughter was pleasing. "One day," I thought, "Others will hear her laughter." They never did, and after my father's death, neither did I. That particular laughter was reserved only for him.

As I lay beneath the layers of blankets and quilts, dreading the run from the heatless bedroom to the oil stove in the living room, then to the kitchen, I listened for the sounds of the street below—sounds of passing cars, storekeepers greeting each other, street brooms and a myriad of other sounds destined to arouse the imagination of a young boy.

By the time I reached the kitchen, my mother's attitude changed from felicity to stoic. The business day had begun. She rarely smiled, never joked (especially in public) and spoke only when she had something important to say. During her lifetime, Nellie never colored outside the lines, maybe a tribute to her early raising or a plague of her past. I never knew. I always colored near the borders and sometimes outside the lines.

When the restaurant opened for the breakfast business, Nellie had baked four pies with four more in the oven and was now preparing the "meat and three" lunch, which would later become the "meat and three" dinner. Meanwhile, my father waited on the early customers, serving coffee and fixing breakfast to order, during the course of which a story or two was exchanged along with the news and the weather.

One of my favorite stories involved Ross Ayers, a distant cousin, who occasionally spent an hour or two or four or an entire Saturday afternoon at one or more of the local beer joints on Railroad Avenue, drinking until he was barely able to walk or talk. You could always tell when Ross was drunk or near drunk because he would start to talk in an intimate whisper.

One Saturday afternoon Ross stopped by the restaurant on his way home, took my father into the kitchen for a private conversation and whispered, "Homer, would you let me have a quart of beer to go. And, could you put the beer on credit." My father smiled and escorted Ross back to the dining room, seated him at the nearest table and returned to the kitchen. In the kitchen, dad blew his breath into an empty paper bag, twisted the top, then returned to the dining room, holding the bag as if it contained a fragile treasure.

My father gently handed the bag to Ross, telling him, "Now Ross, hold one hand under the bag and one hand on top. Don't drop it. You can't open the bag until you get home. Otherwise, you may get me in trouble with the law. And, by the way, this is on the house."

Ross gently carried the bag, holding it as Daddy had instructed, walking out of the restaurant, down the two steps to the street, and south on Monroe Street toward his home. My father and I, joined by three or four customers, ran to the side window for a good look at Ross, slowly staggering out the street holding the bag ever so carefully, just as he was instructed. He never fell or dropped the bag. We could only imagine Ross' surprise when he opened the bag and found it empty. Ross never mentioned the incident, but it became one of my father's favorite stories.

Despite her stoic demeanor and Victorian appearance, I recognized, at an early age, that there was something special about my mother. Over time, I began to realize that my mother was probably the best pie maker in the world—at least in *my* world. Her pies were the reason so many people frequented our family restaurant—pies that would have been featured in any four star restaurant in the outside world. In fact, some customers would travel for miles on the winding, mountain roads for lunch or dinner at the little restaurant and every meal would be topped off with a piece of one of Nellie's pies.

"Nellie, that's about the best pie I ever tasted," remarked a frequent customer who had just finished his second slice of cocoanut pie, after a lunch of roast beef and gravy, mashed potatoes and gravy, green beans, corn, four rolls and a half pot of coffee. It was the second trip that month for the customer and his wife who lived in Beckley, West Virginia, about fifty miles south. They drove the winding roads to our little restaurant for one purpose: for a slice of the best pie they ever tasted.

The customer's total bill was $1.75. As he continued to rave about the pie, he handed my mother a dollar tip. Nellie thanked the customer and lowered her head, seemingly embarrassed by the customer's kind remarks and the large tip. She didn't smile, but then she rarely smiled. Yet, there was a little twinkle in her eyes that said she liked this customer and she liked his remarks.

This scene was repeated numerous times over the years by hundreds of customers, all attesting to the fact that Nellie made the best pies anyone ever tasted. The meringue pies were a favorite— generally cocoanut, chocolate, butterscotch and lemon pies, topped with a mound of meringue, a mixture of egg whites with sugar, beaten until stiff and browned in the oven until the tips of the meringue began to turn brown. Then, there were the fruit pies: apple and peach and my favorite, egg custard. The slice of pie you were eating was the best pie anyone ever tasted, depending, of course, upon which pie you were eating at the time.

I never knew what made a Nellie pie so special. Customers frequently asked Nellie for a recipe, usually for the pie they had just consumed. Always happy to oblige, Nellie, in her matter of fact voice, dictated as the customer wrote—a touch of this, a tad of that and a smidgen of something else. I was always amused. Although Nellie was quite serious, the customer's pie was certain to be a disaster. While the average woman cooks, using measuring spoons, measuring cups, cook books and recipes, Nellie never did.

Nellie's early life, her life before my father, was always something of a mystery. From little tidbits of conversation, I was able to piece together parts of her life, which left large gaps to time—gaps which, for some reason, Nellie didn't want to reveal. I often wondered about what happened in those gaps of time. Sometimes I would press her for answers involving her past life. Most times, she was too busy for those answers, or she would simply change the subject for no obvious reason. Yet, there were rare moments when she would give a terse response, apparently without thinking. It is from those moments that I was able to get a small glimpse of her life.

Nellie was one of fifteen children born to Ed Hunter and Ada Walker Hunter, who farmed a fairly large acreage tract of land on Muddy Creek Mountain, three or four miles northeast of the town of Alderson, West Virginia. In 1907 Ada was bedridden with typhoid fever, leaving her children to the care of Ed, who was adept in making children—not raising them. As a result, the children were parceled out to several benevolent families in the nearby town. Nellie was assigned to the family of Isaac W. Rowe, his wife Hannah B. Rowe, whose younger children, Harry and Fred I., and perhaps their daughter, Lilly, all older than Nellie, were probably still living at home.

So, at the age of ten, this small, frail, frightened girl walked along the dirt road leading from her parental home on Muddy Creek Mountain to the Rowe home in the valley town, carrying all of her worldly possessions, consisting of a few hand-me-down dresses, underclothes, and a rag doll. After that day, she would rarely return to Muddy Creek Mountain. Although she was never restricted by the Rowe family or by anyone else, her new world simply wouldn't allow it.

At the apron of Hannah B. Rowe, Nellie learned to cook and melded into the fastidious lifestyle of the Rowe family, which included their German heritage. She remained in school through the eighth grade, above average for females at that time, and after graduation remained with the Rowe's until her marriage to my father. During this time, she became something of a self-taught pie maker, with the aid of her German mentor. It didn't take much mentoring. She had the gift.

For some reason, I could never adapt to Nellie's lifestyle. As the years passed, from elementary school to junior high then to high school, I continued to distance myself from my mother. It wasn't that I disliked her. We just had nothing in common.

At fourteen, I lied about my age and got a job at the local drug store, working six days a week during the summers and after school, Saturdays and Sunday afternoons during the school year. This was my escape from the restaurant business. Besides, the money gave me a new sense of independence.

Then, in January 1954, after completing one semester at Concord College in Athens, West Virginia, I was left with $15.00 in my pocket and a sense of urgency to move on with my life. I hitchhiked to Beckley, West Virginia, and joined the U. S. Air Force, understanding all the while that my four years in the Air Force would only be a transaction period in my life and that I would later return to college, more mature and with a college stipend from the G.I. Bill. Besides, I could earn some college credits while in the Air Force.

Inside the passenger car of the Chesapeake & Ohio train that would take me from Beckley, West Virginia, to Geneva, New York, then to Sampson Air Force Base for basic training, I joined my faceless brothers, mindlessly staring from window next to my seat —staring at nothing in particular, just the scenery, all of those things that make the background for a railroad trip. After a hundred miles and a few towns had passed, I found myself concentrating on the events of the past day.

That was the day that I announced to my mother and to my sister, Ethel, that I was leaving for the Air Force. Both were evidently dumbfounded or stunned. It was as if I had said, "I'm leaving to get a haircut." Since my announcement didn't elicit much of a response, I told both Nellie and Ethel that I needed to tell my friends goodbye. I walked to the end of the bridge, to Mack's Snack Shack and to the pool room, telling all of my friends of my decision and that I would miss them.

Afterwards, I returned home for my last farewell and to pick up the small athletic bag with an extra change of clothes, shaving equipment and toiletries. At the last minute, as I was ready to walk out the door, my mother threw her arms around my neck, told me she loved me for the first time in my memory, and with tears streaming down her face whispered, "Don't go." I was so shocked that I don't recall what, if anything, I said in response. And, I don't remember leaving. I only remember that scene, recurring over and over in my head, as I started my transition to my new world. While tempted, I knew that I would not return, except for a few days each year or every few years. My new world just wouldn't allow it.

I finally recognized that Nellie and I had more in common than I had ever imagined, and that the umbilical cord binding the mother with her child is never really severed at birth. I also made another startling discovery on that long train ride. I did, indeed, love my mother and she would be the single person that I missed most as I made my way into my new world.

When the train pulled in to Geneva, New York, I sensed that it was time for me to learn how to make my pies. My stove was starting to dance.

www.ingramcontent.com/pod-product-compliance
Lightning Source LLC
LaVergne TN
LVHW021502080426
835509LV00018B/2369